Let Us Give Thanks

A Parish Priest Speaks with his People

– Further Selected Sermons –

Cormac Rigby

FAMILY PUBLICATIONS

OXFORD

ISBN 1-871217-52-0......... (hardback)
ISBN 1-871217-51-2........ (paperback)

by the same author
The Lord be with You
(also available on CD)
Lift Up Your Hearts

*The author and the publishers wish to express their thanks
to those friends and parishioners who kindly allowed
the use of their illustrations in this book.*

*Cover: Cardinal Basil Hume with Fr Cormac
at the ordination of Fr John O'Leary,
at Most Sacred Heart, Ruislip, 14 July 1992.
Photograph by Stephen Patterson*

published by
Family Publications
6a King Street, Oxford, OX2 6DF
www.familypublications.co.uk

printed in England by
Cromwell Press, Trowbridge, Wilts.

Contents

Relaxing in his flat in Summertown, North Oxford, Fr Cormac is surrounded by his books, particularly his comprehensive collection of books on ballet.   *photo: Tony Randall*

About the author

Fr Cormac Rigby is a priest of the Westminster diocese. He has also been an historian of Victorian education, a radio announcer, and a respected writer and broadcaster on ballet.

He was educated at St Theresa's in Rickmansworth, Holy Rood in Watford, and Merchant Taylors'. He was a Sir Thomas White scholar of St John's College, Oxford, where he read Modern History. His doctoral thesis was on the life and influence of the great nineteenth-century teacher, Edward Thring, headmaster of Uppingham 1853–1887.

For twenty years (1965–1985), he was a BBC announcer, the last fourteen of them as Presentation Editor, Radio 3. His deep love of the ballet led to the Radio 3 series *Royal Repertoire*, which ran throughout the 1970s, and to his writing on the ballet for *Dance and Dancers*, *Set to Music*, *The Oxford Mail*, *The Times* and *Dance Now*. He scripted the final programme for *Ballet for All* ('Ashton: The Dream Era') and in 2003 David Bintley dedicated his new ballet *Beauty and the Beast* 'For Cormac'.

Cardinal Basil Hume ordained him on 21 May 1988 and appointed him to be assistant priest at Most Sacred Heart, Ruislip. In 1999 he became Parish Priest of St William of York, Stanmore. He was diagnosed with cancer in 2003 and returned to live in North Oxford.

A collection of his sermons, *The Lord be with You*, was published at the end of 2003 and was so well received that a second and now a third selection have been made.

Introduction

When I came up to Oxford in 1958, I found myself on the same staircase as a chemistry scholar from Merchiston, and he became the most tremendous influence on my life in Oxford and beyond. He had a radio, and a gramophone, and he had all the knowledge of music and theatre that were totally new to me. Part of my growing up was the amount of time that I spent in his room on the first floor on Staircase 19, listening to serious music for the first time in my life.

The influence of John Eccles transformed me. I brought to Oxford a very strong Catholicism that was Irish and Lancastrian. And that by itself simply wasn't enough. I was bright but I was narrow. Those three undergraduate years of John's gentle encouragement were crucial. At the end of them I went off to Rome to study for the priesthood. It lasted less than a year. I found that I was the wrong person, in the wrong place, at the wrong time, which is quite a difficult discovery to make about yourself. And so I came back to St John's and abandoned all thought of priesthood. I returned to become a historian, but then after three years of full-time research, I deviated into broadcasting and spent twenty years there.

Just after I came back to Oxford, in November 1963, John had a car crash and was very seriously injured. The six weeks that I spent at his side in intensive care in Aylesbury were the watershed of my life. There was life before Aylesbury and there was life after. The life before, when I look back on it now, was very knowallish, very priggish, very immature.

In the days after his death on 1st January 1964, I made a vow that I would try to live his life as well as my own life. And as I look back on it now over the long perspective of the years, I see those twenty years I spent from 1965 with Radio 3 as being very much the continuity of his life, and the twenty years I gave to the Church as the continuity of mine. Not as in any sense a sort of

Jekyll and Hyde existence, but as two lives flowing into one. All the great things he contributed to my life and my maturing and my growing up helped me eventually to be a much better priest than I would have been if I had simply gone through the seminary in 1962. He was my morning-star who became after 1964 my beckoning evening-star.

Many people have influenced the way I interpret priesthood, and also, therefore, how I preach sermons. I was a layman for more than twenty years and I heard an awful lot of sermons and I heard an awful lot of awful sermons. But it is very difficult to try to find a voice of your own that is authentic.

It's first of all, for the priest, a sharing of the quest. You know that everyone sitting listening to you is trying to find God, is trying to make a friendship with Christ, trying to deepen their spiritual perception, and so you are sharing with them in that quest. And you are very conscious when you're standing in the pulpit that a great many of them are much deeper and are much further along the road of holiness than you are yourself. You sometimes feel it's almost an impertinence to be preaching.

And yet at the same time it's important, because you've been given a particular knowledge of the Gospel and mandated by the bishop who ordained you to pass it on. That's the imperative: pass it on, share it. You are shedding new light because that's your job, the job of the preacher.

Each person listening is starting from a different place. The one thing that they all have in common – no matter what their IQ, no matter how theologically learned– the one thing they all want is encouragement. And if there's one thing that I try to keep in mind all the way through parish sermons, it is how does this encourage those who hear it to come even closer to God.

This coda of my life is turning out to be one of the most fruitful and happy of all the chapters, and I can't thank Denis and Valerie Riches enough for what they've done to make so much of it so positive and delightful.

Prayer doesn't require great cathedrals or beautiful churches. The University Chaplaincy chapel at Oxford in 1958 was actually a Nissen hut, but efforts had been made to make it feel like a place of prayer. Undergraduates arriving for Mass were able to come into this tranquillity and disengage from the world outside, and kneel in silent adoration before the Real Presence in the tabernacle.

Photo: Brian Harding

Chapter 1

It is because you have not prayed properly.

Do you remember the eclipse of the sun last year?
For a few moments in the middle of the day,
the light diminished, and a strange hush descended
as the birds stopped singing.

It was a curious, almost eerie silence. Like those moments
before a play starts in the theatre. The house-lights dim,
and the audience becomes still, and the curtain rises.

I love that hush of expectation.

In the days when I was announcing live relays on Radio 3
I remember being at Covent Garden. The radio audience,
of course, can't see the house-lights being dimmed. They
are listening to the announcer telling the story of Act I.
But the announcer has agreed a cue with the backstage
management, so that when he reaches a certain point
in the script they will begin to dim the lights and, by
the time he finishes the narration, the theatre audience
will be quiet and the conductor will enter, bang on cue.

On this particular evening I was in the usual box next to
the proscenium and everything was going to plan. But as
I told the story of Act I in a normal voice, a lady in the box
next door heard me still talking as the lights dimmed and
assumed that I was a peasant who knew no better
and leant across, and said very loudly: SHUSH!

In a way she was right. She wasn't to know that we had got
our timings honed to perfection and she was rightly concerned
that some idiot might be going to spoil the opening bars of

the overture. That hush before a performance is a necessity, a preparation to listen.

I love listening to my CDs but there's one huge difference between putting on a CD at home and going to a live performance in a concert hall. At home you press the remote control and the music starts. Just like that. But in the live concert you settle yourself in a comfortable position and conversation dies away, and you hear that most wonderful of all noises, a sound that always thrills me, the sound of an orchestra tuning.

The oboe judges the right moment to give the note and then you hear this glorious cacophony of preparation and adjustment. Your ear may pick out the clarinet trying out his big tune from the second movement, or the timps having a last run at a tricky exposed passage in the finale. The sound is the sound of concentration – of people focusing their attention on what matters. And their preparation helps the audience do the same.

Starting a Beethoven symphony on CD is like switching on the light – boo boo boo boom. There it is. Instant. But in the proper context you are getting ready as the players themselves get ready.

The period of tuning gets players and audience into a concentrated frame of mind so that all are *ready* to listen. And I believe we need that in church too.

The silence in church before Mass is the period of preparation, the tuning of our minds. And we need to help ourselves by respecting that silence.

When we come in to the precincts of the church it's great to greet our neighbours cheerfully; when we come into the porch we can say hello and catch up on urgent information. But once

we come into the church itself and genuflect
to Our Lord in the tabernacle and kneel in our place
then we are in the period of preparation for the
great miracle of the Mass.

The attitude we adopt not only reflects our respect
for God's house and for the Lord in the tabernacle,
but our considerateness towards our fellow-worshippers
as they prepare themselves for Mass.

It used to be the case that when you went to non-Catholic
churches, people sat and chatted till the service began
whereas in Catholic churches people knelt in prayerful
silence and respect, tuning up for the Mass. It grieves me
when Catholics fail to respect that period of preparation.

Yes, of course, occasionally something *must* be said, but
one tries to say it in a whisper. When I come through
the church I don't want to seem unfriendly – but a silent
wave, or nod of the head is enough. The quiet intensification
of prayer before Mass is important for all of us. Chat on the
way out when Mass is over, but before Mass we need, we really need
to leave distractions outside and give ourselves to silence.

The forecourt and the porch are the places for cheerful chatter
but once inside the House of God let us pray, let us concentrate,
let us bring our minds to order and focus on the great symphony
of God's love.

Let's make a resolution now that each of us will do the best
we can to help everyone else by preserving the silence in church,
and preparing for the miracle that is about to happen.
It is so loving to one's neighbour,
it is so respectful towards the Real Presence
to create that atmosphere of expectation and concentration
in the silence of God's house before Mass.

Let us pray properly.

St John the Baptist

"John is the first step to Jesus."

Picture by Raphael (1483–1520) in the Galleria dell' Academia, Florence.

Chapter 2

A man came, sent by God. His name was John.

John is the morning star: the light that sparkles
so brilliantly in the darkest hour before the dawn,
and then in that wondrous rosy light of the sunrise.

In the full radiance of the morning we tend to forget
the morning star which was our first awareness of light,
our first indicator, our first love.

I frequently thank God for the beginnings
of my faith and for the beginning of love.
The two go together: love and faith.
Faith is not often an intellectual breakthrough:
it is more usually a consequence of love.
Love comes first – and love gives insights,
deeper perceptions of our existence which produce
intimations of faith. Love opens the eyes to faith –
and faith then demands to understand more fully.

Our task as believers is that of *fides quaerens intellectum:*
faith seeking understanding. I am sure that there are
some people who can argue their way to belief in God:
they look at the world and deduce a creator;
they look at creation and discern pattern and purpose.
But I suspect that they are fairly rare.
Faith is not usually the conclusion of an intellectual journey.

How did faith evolve? In the beginning man lived
in a fearful world, outside of Eden, full of unpredictable
and often threatening powers.

Our remote ancestors thought it wise to placate those powers
and keep them at a safe distance.

It was not so much a faith in many gods as fear of many unknowns.
Later, when man had survived for long enough
to recognise the beauty of the world and to perceive
the potential of humanity, an awareness began to stir –
that the unknown powers in the world are not necessarily
baleful and menacing but may be benevolent and good.

Maybe, they thought, the world is a combat zone where
growth and flowering contend against decay and death.
Maybe life is just picking a way through a minefield of
hazards, hoping for survival. But eventually, those ideas
of good gods fighting bad gods gradually died away.

Men of insight began to see that the one real power
is the one that stands behind all natural phenomena:
their Creator, and that therefore

    Our destiny, our being's heart and home
    Is with infinitude, and only there.

Wordsworth expressed it in various ways. He felt

    A presence that disturbs me with the joy
    Of elevated thoughts; a sense sublime
    Of something far more deeply interfused,
    Whose dwelling is the light of setting suns,
    And the round ocean and the living air,
    And the blue sky, and in the mind of man.

A destiny for man, and a presence that disturbs.
But is that enough?

Humanity, unaided, can get no further
than some distant spirit of benevolence – like Wordsworth –
or some all-too-close spirit of judgment –
like the God of the Old Testament.

And God saw that those two notions were inadequate,
because what God actually *is*, is LOVE.

And this is what he had to reveal about himself –
by taking on a human nature himself.

The Word was made flesh and dwelt among us.
For the first time
it was not fear of the unknown or fear of retribution,
it was not intellectual curiosity or poetic fancy
that drew people to God,
but the perception that God is Love.

How? Jesus.
Jesus, preaching and teaching and healing
Jesus, bravely challenging worldly power
Jesus, suffering for his beliefs
Jesus, sacrificing life itself for love
Jesus, risen from the grave.

Jesus makes the invisible God visible.
Love is made incarnate and draws to itself
the instinct to love that exists in all of us.

How do we know love? By our experience of being loved.
The most wonderful experience of human life
is knowing we are loved.
By parents, initially,
by siblings, family, friends,
and then perchance by the One Significant Other.

It's not something you can deduce logically.
You just know when you are loved.
Love speaks heart to heart –
it speaks the deepest truths, and often without words.
We can all echo the truth in that magical song from
Guys and Dolls: 'I'll know when my love comes along.'

Love looks at the world with different eyes.
Love gives a different sort of understanding.
You don't begin with understanding and then go on to love.

No, you experience love and then seek understanding.
It's love, made visible in Jesus, that opens our hearts
and then our minds to understanding.

John saw Him coming.
John the Baptist was the summit of the old perceptions –
and then he saw, coming towards him, a man he recognised
as the one who would offer himself in sacrifice,
and whom he therefore described as the Lamb of God.

His own task was to be the witness,
to proclaim that morning was about to break
and that the Risen Son of God would totally transform
our faith and perceptions.

You look at the babe in the manger and bless God
for taking on such helplessness.
You look at Christ on the Cross and your heart overflows
with love for the God who endured so much.

Jesus is love personified.

John is the first step to Jesus
and Jesus
is the great leap of understanding
that says we are immortal diamond
because He died for us.

   I am all at once what Christ is,
       since he was what I am, and
  This Jack, joke, poor potsherd,
      patch, matchwood, immortal diamond,
        Is immortal diamond.

Gerard Manley Hopkins

Chapter 3

You entrusted me with five talents.

I don't think this Gospel reading is about investment,
savings accounts, interest rates, Tessas and such like.
Prudent handling of money is always a good idea,
of course, but what we're talking about here is
our gifts, our characteristics, our abilities, our potential.
We were made for a purpose and if we truly believe that,
then it is vital to suss out what that purpose is.

The phrase 'personal fulfilment' comes to mind.
Yes, says twenty-first century man, life is a challenge
for every individual and the key to success
is meeting all the challenges of life.

And so we turn our lives into a series of assessments.
Life is one long continuous assessment and those who
succeed are those whose CV is most impressive and
whose salaries indicate their value in the market-place.

The problem with that view of life is that it is
entirely wrapped up in the self. It evaluates the
person in terms of achievements and market value.
It is not a Christian perception.

So how does Christianity see the purpose of life?
It looks first at God and sees that God is love.
And then it looks at his creation and realises that
creation is motivated by love. And then it looks
at those who have been created in God's love
and concludes that their purpose must be to love.

If we are made in the image of God,
and God's essential being is love,

then we are most truly fulfilled when we love.
And love is the giving of self to other.

Now that makes quite a difference to how we see
the purpose of life. Our assessment is no longer
does he live well? But does he love well?

What do I mean by love?
Do I mean romantic love and affection?
Well, yes, of course. That sort of experience
is absolutely essential because it shows us *how* to love.
The love we feel intuitively for our friends becomes
the touchstone by which we can measure the love
we know we have to give to all.

We have favourites — that's only human;
God doesn't — that's divine.
But if we use the experience of loving our favourites
to show us how to love all, then we walk
in the steps of Jesus. We are specifically told how
deeply he loved his friends, notably John and Lazarus.

Jesus laughs at us when we fail to see the point.
Well of course it's easy to love, he says, if you love
the good and the beautiful and those who love you back —
even out-and-out heathens can do that!

What we have to do is to learn from that experience and
to love all equally and with that same urgent determination.
And that brings us back to that story of the talents.
I think it means 'opportunities'.

Each day brings us opportunities to love,
to behave in loving ways, to think loving thoughts,
to turn away from selfishness and choose generosity instead.

Today I may be given five talents,
five unlooked-for, unexpected opportunities,
to show goodness of heart, to show understanding and perception,

to show kindness and affection,
to show the good humour of Christ.
And if I ignore any one of those five chances,
I waste part of my life's purpose.
The really sad human being is the little person so wrapped-up
in himself that he denies any opportunities exist.
"I know you want me to be a saint", he says,
"but I couldn't find any scope for heroic sanctity today
so I sat at home and did nothing."
And he forgets that the real saint is the one who sees every day
filled with moments of choice, filled with opportunities.

Every thing we do can be done for love if we choose.
No one else needs to know.
Do I hurt? "Offer it up", said my mother.
Spot on. Dealing with suffering can be made an act of love.

Do I create a good atmosphere?
It's not the signing of large cheques for good causes
that proves love. It's the climate of affection
and the proliferation of tiny kindnesses.
Even the way I answer the phone can be an act of love,
even the way I am courteous to strangers.

Five talents, two talents, one talent.
Five opportunities, two opportunities, one opportunity.
Opportunities to open the eyes of someone else
to the love of God in the world.

There isn't an aspect of me that can't be turned
to a good purpose; even my faults enable me
to understand and love someone who shares those faults.

Life is not a continuous assessment. Life is one
long wonderful sequence of opportunities to love.
The truly gifted, the truly talented, are those who
never miss an opportunity to love.

"Oberon was magnificent … It wasn't someone else I was inventing, but me as Oberon"

Kevin O'Hare as Oberon in Sir Frederick Ashton's ballet, *The Dream*. (Birmingham Royal Ballet). *Photo: Jimmy Wormser*

Chapter 4

There is a small boy here with five barley loaves and two fish.

I wonder who he was, and if he grew up to be a Christian.
I wonder why he happened to be in that crowd, and why he
was the only one sensible enough to have brought some food.
Perhaps he'd set off on some magical mystery tour of his own,
and somehow got caught up in events.

I did similar things when I was a small boy. I'd put some food
in my saddle-bag and pedal off to Chesham or Amersham or
Windsor – wherever the fancy took me. On my bike it wasn't
boring like the bus. In my imagination it wasn't leafy Bucks,
but Sherwood Forest or the Forest of Arden. It wouldn't have
surprised me to bump into Robin Hood or Oberon and Titania.
At that age you invent your own journeys and your own
scenarios, and they are even more real than reality.

In the book cupboards in the back room were a couple of
sets of volumes of condensed classics, beautifully illustrated.
I loved them. I can still see a scene from *A Midsummer
Night's Dream*: deep in the forest, a grove where the King
and Queen of the Fairies were normally seen in amity together,
but on this occasion squabbling.

Oberon was magnificent, extravagantly and impressively dressed
and Titania was absolutely beautiful. And I was Oberon.
I imagined myself going through the actions of the story and
I could imagine storylines that Shakespeare never thought of.
It wasn't someone else I was inventing but me as Oberon.
I look back at it now with some amusement; I find myself
less credible as Oberon these days. But how important was
that long ago flight of the imagination.

It's one of the most crucial experiences of childhood, not just to listen to stories but to create our own and to be their protagonist. It's a stretching of the imagination, not accommodating grown-ups' ideas but discovering our own. Children have this wonderful time of experiencing no limits to what is possible.

If Oberon could be invisible, I could be invisible. If Oberon could wander at will through the Forest of Arden, so could I. It is in this guileless fantasising that small human beings discover what it is to be someone else. They are learning the great art of human perception, being able to put themselves inside someone else's skin, to see life with someone else's eyes. I was actually deepening my humanity by imagining what it must be like to be Oberon, or Puck, or Oliver Twist, or Snow White's Prince – or even Bambi or Tarka the Otter.

I vividly remember my Mother reading *A Tale of Two Cities*, that exciting story of the French Revolution where one of the doomed aristocrats had a double, a rather seedy English lawyer. For the sake of the Frenchman's wife and child, Sidney Carton was prepared to go to the guillotine in his place: "It is a far, far better thing that I do than I have ever done."

If I couldn't be Oberon, maybe I could be Sidney Carton. It was certainly Sidney Carton who opened my soul to the idea of redemption.

What children are learning is how to put themselves into someone else's shoes, and that is the beginning of real love, the imaginative understanding of someone else. In a word, empathy. And that's something we must learn and never forget. The horrors of our world occur so often because people can't imagine what it's like to be someone else.

We shut ourselves up inside our own realities and close our minds to other people's realities. We lock ourselves into our self-sufficient complacency and heartlessness and we fail to see what it is like to be as others really are.

George Bernard Shaw had one of his characters say at the end of *Saint Joan*: "Must then a Christ perish in torment in every age to save those who have no imagination?"

The realities of life need an active empathy, an open heart. People content to wallow in their own inglorious mud are unreal, whereas the use of imagination in the theatre creates a real world of the understanding heart. It is awareness of the realities of others that opens the heart to love.

The unreal world is built on selfishness. The real world is the realm of empathy. Children *know* that and we must never forget it. This is what Jesus meant on that famous occasion when he set a little child in front of them and said "Unless you become as little children, you will never enter the kingdom." He didn't mean he wanted us to be childish and immature, but to preserve and deepen that willingness to imagine what it's like to be someone else.

Next week we're having a special collection for the Catholic Children's Society. They call it their Bucket and Spade Appeal to help disadvantaged children. They take them for a holiday by the sea, to open their eyes to the magic of the waves and to build sandcastles, and maybe to imagine what it's like to be a mermaid, or a water-baby, or a whale – or a Filipino seaman, or an offshore fisherman. It's opening the eyes of children to see the world afresh and to learn how to love by using their imagination.

During his undergraduate years, 1958–61, Fr Cormac went to daily Mass, usually at 7.15 am, in the Jesuit church of St Aloysius.

In those days it was normal in parishes where several priests were in residence for each of them to say Mass. On many occasions, while one Mass was being said at the main altar, Cormac would be serving another being said simultaneously at the Lady Altar.

Chapter 5

All generations will call me blessed.

I was only eleven for the Holy Year of 1950,
but I remember when the Pope – Pius XII – defined
the dogma of the Assumption. And I was old enough
to make sense of it when it was explained to me.

I knew that when we die we are either buried or cremated.
Our body has worn out – or whatever – and so we discard it.
Our soul – the real reality of who we are – continues to exist,
in a new dimension. But we don't see the body again until
we are reunited on the Last Day.

I remember the old song:

> John Brown's body lies a-mouldering in the grave,
> But his soul goes marching on.

So I was happy with the idea that, when we die,
the essential bit of us flies free, and the accidental bit of us –
which causes us so much hassle – has to be put on hold
until it reappears at the Resurrection on the Last Day.

The death of the body is "the blight man was born for".
No exceptions, but one. And I'd learnt all about that,
not from the Pope's new dogma, but from the Rosary.
The fourth Glorious Mystery: the assumption of Our Lady
into heaven. And I'd seen several of Titian's beautiful paintings
of Mary going up into heaven.
It seemed to me entirely right and proper that Mary –
who had been such a perfect Mother to Jesus –
should have special provision made for her.

The rest of us need to go to heaven via purgatory, but not Mary.
She had nothing to repent, nothing to regret. So when her turn
came to die it wasn't like every other death. No dwindling
into dust for her. She could be resurrected at the very moment
of her last breath.

I discovered later that the Orthodox churches don't refer
to Mary's death, but to her 'dormition' – her going to sleep.
Death has no sting for her. She breathed her last and was
then assumed into heaven. And at the end of the Rosary
that wonderful event was celebrated in heaven:
the Mother of Christ the King was crowned queen.
You can deduce that very easily.

Now is this just a pretty devotional picture of a super saint?
Of course not. It goes much deeper. As so often,
the Church evolved its understanding of the mysteries
of the faith through prayer.

The fourth Glorious Mystery of the Rosary was proclaiming
the Assumption five hundred years before Pope Pius XII
defined it. It's one of those developments of doctrine
which follows the logic of other teachings.

If Mary was specially prepared by God to enable the incarnation
to take place, if the Son of God had no human father – only
a human mother – then the human nature of Jesus had to come
entirely from the Virgin Mary. She was created, in the usual way,
by her parents. But God preserved her from any contact with sin.
She was – in her own words to Bernadette at Lourdes –
the Immaculate Conception. If she was then born without sin
and lived without sin, it follows that when she came to die,
sin had no hold over her. She was assumed into heaven;
her bodily resurrection was the first and most perfect
of all bodily resurrections.

The deductive theology which worked it all out began
with Augustine, Albert the Great, Aquinas and Bonaventure.
The Dominicans encouraged the idea in the devotional
context of the Rosary. In the eighteenth century,
Pope Benedict XIV declared it a "probable opinion".

So in 1950, Pius XII wasn't inventing a new concept;
he was summing up and validating a fully developed
insight into the working of salvation. And, of course,
it is a pointer to something else: what happened to Mary
two thousand years ago will be what happens to us
in the fullness of time.

She needed no posthumous purification. We do.
And when we are purified, then we will become as
fully human as Mary our Mother.

Jesus, the Son of God and Son of Man had the divine power
to rise from the dead himself. The whole of humanity
had to be redeemed by the self-sacrifice of Jesus –
and the first of the redeemed is Mary.
A human being, like ourselves, body and soul,
in eternity. Where she was assumed, we hope to follow.

Human beings eternalized.
That's the awesome truth we celebrate today.

The Ascension of Christ
was the divine act of resurrection completed.
Easter Sunday leads inevitably to Ascension Thursday.

Mary was human – not divine. A creature like ourselves,
but without any contamination. And there she is:
our human Mother waiting for us to join her in eternity.

The Ascension of our Lord is a divine feast.
The Assumption of our Lady is a human feast,
to gladden all our hearts.

I love the way the mediaeval mystery plays portrayed the
Assumption. The National Theatre production a few years ago
didn't see Mary as the beautiful young girl painted by Titian.
It saw her as a gentle grey-haired mother who'd been carefully
looked after by John after the death of Jesus. There she was:
a little, almost frail, smiling old lady.

And when she went to sleep, Christ her Son strode down
from heaven to meet his Mother and escort her into
the Kingdom. She was dressed in a neat blue suit
with a simple necklace, and like every good woman,
she wouldn't dream of going anywhere – even to heaven –
without her large, blue, soft leather handbag.

Chapter 6

The Lord is compassion and love.

For Christians, love is the key to understanding –
understanding ourselves and how we tick –
understanding the world and how we relate to it.
But how do we approach the idea of love?

We're familiar with the idea that there are two
great commandments:

> Love the Lord thy God
> Love thy neighbour as thyself.

But be honest, when I said that, did it sound exciting?
Did it make your heart beat faster?

Love is exciting isn't it? An affair of the heart?
A feeling, a sensation, a wonderful experience
that really switches us on and keeps us going?

Well, yes, it is and it's very important to be aware of that.
There's nothing wrong with falling in love and being in love.
But how does it relate to love of God and love of neighbour?
Does it relate at all? Or are they completely separate things?

Let's start with the basics. Our prime purpose and our first duty
is to love God. It was God who gave us life and so it is natural
for us to love our creator. God is both Father and Mother to us
and so we love God in return as naturally and as trustingly
as we would love an ideal human father and mother.
It's an ongoing task and an ever–deepening delight
to explore that relationship with God our parent.

We tend to begin, like children do, saying we love God because
that's what we're *supposed* to do. But as life goes on we love God

because we discover he's lovely, and loving to us and because
in the person of Jesus he is so loveable and so beautiful.
The closer one comes to Jesus, the more sense life makes.

So, first and foremost, love God, who made us.
And then 'love thy neighbour as thyself.'
Why? Because it follows logically.

Upstairs I've got a cushion-cover, framed, which my mother
spent hours embroidering. I love it because she *made* it.
And so, if the God I love has made other things
and other people, it's natural for me to love
what he has made because he made it.

So I begin by loving my creator because he gave me life
and I go on to love my fellow-creatures because he loves them.
And then, last but not least, I love myself because I'm aware
that he has made me as I am.

He loves me uniquely, he fashioned me, and cherished me
and when I made a mess of things he was ready to pick me up
and put me on my feet again. God loves me. So I don't need
to be worried about loving myself, warts and all.

It's rather sad when people can't accept themselves as they are
and can't love themselves. I remember when I was a teenager,
I was a bit self-conscious about my nose, which seemed
far too big and ugly. I mentioned it rather bitterly one day
to the one who loved me. And he simply laughed and said,
Nonsense! It's a nice nose! And because *he* liked it,
I came to like it myself.

Because God loves me as I am, I can love me too, as I am.
And that's how love works: I perceive that I have value in
His eyes. And the real purpose of human relationships is
to give value to other people.

Love takes many forms but the best definition is always
to want, *really* want, the best for the other person:
and that can often mean sacrifice.

If you stopped someone in the street and asked what love is,
they might well say that love is wanting someone, maybe even
wanting someone so much that it hurts. But when you
think about it, that's not love; that's selfishness.
Love is not wanting someone, but wanting the best
for someone. And that is how *God* loves.

I love the idea that Jesus presents himself as the
ardent bridegroom eager to do all he can for the one he loves.
Full of compassion. And love. There is such joy in being
loved by someone you really love. And there's never any
danger in it provided you meet that one essential criterion:
that love isn't wanting someone but wanting absolutely
what is best for that person. And you have to be very clear
about that. What is best for the person I love could be my
frequent presence with them – great! But it could also
mean that I have to make myself scarce – and that's the
really hard one. If I am to ring true as a lover, I have to be
where I'm wanted, *when* I'm wanted
and not where and when I want to be.

Love has to eclipse selfishness
and if it does it will open up new paths to happiness.
Let's set it out very simply:
God is love, and so the first priority is to love Love.
Then to love the people Love has loved to create.
Then to love myself as his creation
and to train myself to see as he sees, and to love as he loves:
and that is a lifetime's vocation
and the most fulfilling of human joys.

PIE JESU, DOMINE

DONA EI REQUIEM

In the first half of the twentieth century the centrality of the Mass in Catholic spiritual life was beyond question.

An Ordination card (for Fr Patrick P Doyle, ordained in Upholland on 21 May 1932) and a Memory card (for Fr John Cooley, who was killed by enemy action at sea, 16 January 1942) both show the Elevation of the Sacred Host, leading our awareness to the Lamb of God, Christ on the Cross.

Chapter 7

You must come away to some lonely place.

We all know that milk is available whenever we want it,
in the supermarkets. And these days supermarkets are open
seven days a week. What a wonderful world we live in:
blessed be Sainsburys and Tesco and Waitrose;
we need never run out of milk again.
But that's just the end product. Where does it come from?

Even the most hyper of supermarkets find a day or two when
they close. But a dairy farmer has to milk his cows every
single day, come rain or come shine. That is a fact of natural life.
And it is one we have to transpose into our spiritual lives.

Man tries very hard to organise his life so that he can safeguard
his days off. Think of the shift patterns and the holiday rosters
that dominate so many of our lives. Man needs his days of rest.
And so there is a constant tension between man the labourer,
who needs his days off, and man the merchant who wants
his sale-points open as long and as profitably as possible.
Either way it is a recurring human problem.

Nature is different. Nature doesn't operate on a basis of five
days on and two days off. Nature doesn't know the difference
between Sunday morning and Monday morning. Nature
operates day by day. The cows have to be milked whichever
day it is. There is no Bank Holiday for the dawn chorus.
And so it is natural, in the most obvious sense of the word,
for us to think 'day by day.' Each and every day has things
that must be done, and one of them is thanking God.

I have a day off every week – by which I mean an away-day,
out of range of telephones and all the rest of it. But that day off
can only begin *after* the essentials. I wouldn't want to have

a day off from saying Mass. That wouldn't be a day of rest, but a day of starvation, a day of deprivation.

The Mass is not part of a job that can be time-tabled only in so-called 'free time'. The Mass is part of nature, a daily-bread sort of happening, a milking-the-cows sort of routine: essentially and naturally daily.

Yes, I know the commandments say it is our duty to keep holy one day in the seven – what I'm saying is that love tells us that it is our privilege to keep holy every single day of our lives. Once we've been to Mass on Sunday we've obeyed the law and fulfilled the demands of the rota. But daily Mass is the call of nature, the privilege of love, the nourishing of the soul. Not a duty, not a chore, but an act of love.

By and large, lovers don't regulate their time together like shift patterns. They long for one another's company. A day without the presence of the one I love is an impoverished day. And so the routine of religious in monasteries and convents, the routine of priests ensures that Mass is there day by day. And I would say that the single most important decision I ever made, thirty years before I became a priest, was to go to Mass every day. And the happiest thing about my fifteen years of priesthood is that there hasn't been a single day when I've been prevented from saying Mass.

I often count my blessings but there's no blessing more sustaining than to be day by day in the presence of Christ as he offers himself to the Father in that agony of love, aching to achieve the forgiveness of all his fellow human beings. I'm not saying a priest is a superhuman who doesn't need a break – on the contrary, every priest needs occasional release from his work. But the Mass isn't work. The Mass is support and strength and food and oxygen. And it wouldn't be a holiday – a holy day – if the Mass were missing from it. It would be as un-natural as leaving the cows unmilked.

Let's think about those events in Mark's Gospel. Christ's
first lot of priests came back shattered from their first preaching
assignments; so Jesus says rest awhile – come away to a
lonely place. He doesn't say go to a lonely place. He says
come to a lonely place, with him. There is his restoring presence.
And in the boat they have the time they needed
to be alone with him.

When they landed, the sheep were there before them and
Jesus simply shrugs: There we go again, and sets himself
to teach them. It's not the hoped-for lonely place that
is significant, it's the travelling to it with Jesus on board.
They discover there is a balance to be kept. Work and rest.
Hurly-burly and retreat. With the sheep – and with God.

Our Christian life is balanced between activity and contemplation.
It is a rhythm of balance: the involvement with humanity,
the dependence on God. The two activities are not
mutually exclusive. You have to expect that when you reach
the lonely place, the people will have got there first.
And you realise that the period of dependence on God is not
a watertight retreat but the journey with Jesus on board.

That's our daily time of prayer and meditation, the quality
time with our creator, not part of our work but an essential
part of our life. For the priest in particular, it is the Mass –
the quality time – that has the quality of eternity. Not a
day without the Mass, is his privilege, not a day without
the Shepherd, not a day's work without that privileged journey
with Jesus on board.

The privilege of the priest is to have that natural rhythm of
daily Mass – and happy the layman or laywoman who can
share with the priest that daily presence of Jesus,
on the altar, on the Cross, at Mass.

Fr Cormac was Parish Priest of St William of York Stanmore from 1999 to 2003. He encouraged devotion to the patronal saint by preaching · about him and printing the text in the parish newsletter, which carried this portrait in its masthead.

It is a photo of part of a stained glass window in Holy Trinity, Brook Green, by Mayer of Munich. St William protects, with his blessing, people thrown into the river Ouse when a bridge collapsed while he was being restored to York.

Chapter 8

We must therefore choose someone.

But it is not always as easy as that. Particularly when the
business of choosing is complicated by spin-doctors who
are prepared to slander rival candidates. One of the most
tragic victims of slander by people who were apparently
well-motivated, but actually seriously misinformed was
our patron saint, William of York.

His name was William Fitzherbert, and I suppose these days
we'd describe him as a junior royal. He was the great-grandson
of William the Conqueror and nephew of King Stephen.
His noble birth gave him a certain advantage – he was
a kind, amiable, easygoing sort of young fellow,
and when he became a priest, it wasn't long before
he was appointed to be chaplain to King Stephen.

But he wasn't a chinless wonder – he had real abilities
as well as a genuinely holy character, and in the 1130s
he became Canon and Treasurer of York Minster.
He did so well in that capacity that it wasn't altogether
surprising that when the Archbishop of York died,
William Fitzherbert was elected to succeed him by
a majority of the chapter.

Unfortunately, his easygoing personality and his noble birth
made him an object of acute suspicion in certain quarters.
It was the time when the austere and zealous Cistercians
had been inspired by St Bernard of Clairvaux to spearhead
a spiritual revival and moral rejuvenation in the Church.
They were very puritanical – you might say judgmental.
They tended to look with a jaundiced eye on anyone
who failed to share this concentrated idealism.

They had their own preferred candidate to be Archbishop: Henry Murdac, a protégé of St Bernard, who was now Abbot of Fountains Abbey. So they resisted William's appointment and accused him of being unworthy. They alleged that he had tried to buy office and that he had been guilty of unchastity and they begged the Archbishop of Canterbury not to consecrate him.

Archbishop Theobald didn't know who to believe; but in any case both sides appealed to Rome, to Pope Innocent II. The Holy Father refused to be brow-beaten by the zealots and decreed in 1143 that it would be OK to go ahead with William's consecration if both he and the Dean of York were prepared to swear an oath that they had not been guilty of simony – the sin of buying a spiritual office.

The most powerful and respected English churchman of the time was Henry of Blois, bishop of Winchester, who was also King Stephen's younger brother. Henry was a conscientious reformer who had been inspired by the Benedictine community of Cluny. He was for forty-five years both Abbot of Glastonbury and Bishop of Winchester. In 1135 he had actually crowned his brother Stephen as King of England. He didn't have the same clout as the Archbishop of Canterbury, until in 1139 he was made papal legate – the Pope's ambassador in England. He was vexed that Theobald of Canterbury had been persuaded not to support William of York. After an enquiry into all the circumstances, Henry of Winchester used his authority as papal legate to consecrate William himself. And so it looked as if the matter was settled.

William embarked on his duties as archbishop and for a couple of years ruled the diocese conscientiously. But his opponents were implacable and after four years he still hadn't received the pallium, the vestment which appears on all archbishops' coats of arms, and is the symbol of papal approval.

So William had to go to Rome in person and sell some of the treasures of York to pay for the journey. Unfortunately there had been changes at the top of the Church. A new pope, Eugenius III, was the first Cistercian to reach the chair of Peter. He had actually been a monk at Clairvaux under Bernard, and was forever receiving trenchant letters of advice from his former boss. Bernard had completely swallowed the line taken by William's opponents and dashed off a series of vituperative letters to popes and legates attacking William.

Those were rough and violent times and the situation was further complicated by the fact that the Pope wasn't able to remain resident in Rome.

After his election as Pope in 1145, in the middle of a civil war, Eugenius had to make his escape even before he was consecrated. He went to Viterbo and then wandered in France for several years, holding councils at Paris, Trier and Rheims – and commissioning St Bernard to preach the second crusade.

Poor William of York didn't stand a chance with all these circumstances stacked against him. Pope Eugenius suspended him until such time as the former Dean of York, now Bishop of Durham, could come to the papal court to swear that William had been elected legitimately.

That rebuff by the Pope went down like a lead balloon with some of William's supporters. They set out to attack Fountains Abbey where the rival candidate was Abbot and largely destroyed it. Their violence was counterproductive; it angered the Pope so much that at the Council of Rheims in 1147 he deposed William altogether, sacked him and appointed Abbot Murdac in his place. William was unable to return to York. Instead, he took refuge with his uncle and protector, Henry of Blois, and lived with great austerity as a simple monk in Winchester.

And there he showed what he was really made of. Not a man of ambition and jealousy, plotting revenge, but a good-natured and holy man who shrugged his shoulders at the harshness of fate and the injustice of slander, and got on with his life.

For some five years, William of York lived in obscurity until in 1153, all his opponents died within a few weeks. Bernard of Clairvaux died, and so did his disciple, Pope Eugenius. And so did Henry Murdac, whom they had forced on York. The new pope, Anastasius IV, was a very old man, but experienced and shrewd. He was able to live safely in Rome and to be an effective Pope. He was a patron of Nicholas Breakspear, the able English monk from St Albans who was to succeed him as Pope: the one and only English Pope.

Maybe Breakspear was able to brief him about the real situation in England. When the news of Murdac's death reached Rome, Pope Anastasius resolved the dispute which had raged for so long over York. He re-appointed William Fitzherbert as archbishop and sent him the pallium.

At long last the gentle William was able to return to York. As a vast procession entered the city in May 1154, one of the bridges over the Ouse collapsed under the weight of the throng and it was said that it was William's prayers that saved every one of them from death.

The newly-restored Archbishop promised restitution to Fountains Abbey and won the respect and love of his people. It was therefore a terrible shock when only a week after his triumphal return, Archbishop William had just finished saying mass, when he collapsed in terrible pain and died.

Such a shock that there were rumours he'd been poisoned.

He was buried with great solemnity in York Minster and people came flocking to his tomb. So many wonderful things happened that fifty years later, Pope Honorius II appointed two churchmen to inquire into his life and miracles. By a curious irony, the two investigators were the Cistercian abbots of Fountains and Rievaulx. They made amends for the misjudgments by their predecessors and advised the Pope that William had been a true saint.

In 1227 St William of York was canonised and a shrine built to house his bones in York Minster. Two centuries on, in 1421, his reputation was still so strong that they erected the wonderful St William window in the Minster, showing no fewer than sixty-two scenes from his life. Behind me, at the foot of the crucifix, you see the initials G.E. – William of York in its Latin form, Guglielmus Eboracensis, and between them the mitre; the symbol of a bishop's office which was worthily acquired, tragically snatched away and briefly restored.

How could such things happen? Those who campaign for *new* causes can often be very intolerant of everyone else. The advocates of the New Monasticism had on their side one of history's greatest spin-doctors, St Bernard of Clairvaux. But the spin against William of York was a terrible misjudgement.

I would hope that when St William died so suddenly, on 8 June 1154, there was someone else besides St Peter to meet him at the gates of heaven. I hope that St Bernard of Clairvaux was there too. To apologise for rushing to judgment and to acknowledge that his attacks on as gentle a saint as William of York had been a terrible mistake. I'm quite sure St William had forgiven him.

Chapter 9

Mary set out and went as quickly as she could.

Some people give to grab attention, to demand gratitude,
to place under an obligation. Those aren't gifts;
they're bribes, and they should be firmly ignored.

The essence of good giving is to know instinctively and
accurately what the recipient would really and genuinely like.
And usually it's not gifts but time, not presents but presence.

Take today's Gospel. Elizabeth – a very elderly lady –
is very unexpectedly pregnant and her much younger cousin
Mary hears the news. Mary doesn't order a Rolls Royce
perambulator from the catalogue! She doesn't sit down
and knit some bootees in colours that exactly match her
own boudoir curtains! No – her cousin needs a hand and so
Mary, although going through the morning sickness patch
herself, sets off as quickly as she can to be of practical help.
It really is as simple as that. What really made old Elizabeth
glad to see her wasn't expensive gifts or show-off generosity
but a helping hand and welcome company.

It's worth bearing that in mind at Christmas. There's an
awful lot of loneliness around, which presents despatched
from a safe distance make worse still. It's the presence
of a warm and friendly human being, rather than presents
from a distant Lady Bountiful that reflects the true spirit
of Christmas. Presence rather than presents.

The real generosity of Christmas has got very little
to do with money – it's measured in the goodness of the heart.

God loves a cheerful giver. Let me tell you a story.
It happened years ago – roughly the time of the early Tudors.
There were two talented young art students, great friends,
Bert and Frank. They didn't come from well-off homes
and they knew that if they wanted to develop their talents
as painters they'd have to graft for it. Students needed to be
apprenticed in the studio of an established master, learning
how to mix colours, how to prepare a canvas as well as how
to cope with perspective, and so on. They'd be at work from
sunrise to sunset – and that's not easy if you've got to earn
your keep as well.

Both Bert and Frank had managed to get part-time jobs
as labourers but it wasn't enough and it took up too much time.
So the two lads made a pact. They decided to draw lots.
The winner would devote all his time to his studies, and start a career.
The one who lost would put his studies on hold and work
full-time as a labourer to earn enough for both of them.

Bert was the winner and got himself apprenticed to a great
master and studied assiduously in his studio. He promised
Frank that when he was established as an artist, he'd then
be able to earn enough from commissions to keep the pair
of them while Frank in his turn launched on *his* training.
It took a number of years for Bert to master the art of drawing
and painting and to be able to receive commissions from rich
clients. But eventually Bert was established and the moment
came when Frank could stop labouring and start his own studies.

But during those years of hard work something had happened
which neither of them had foreseen. Frank's fingers had been
so calloused and bent by all the hard physical labour that
when he tried to pick up an artist's brush and control it with
the necessary delicacy he just couldn't. Frank realised that
he'd never now be able physically to be an artist on a par
with Bert.

Bert was horrified by what had happened
but the damage was done: nothing he could do.

You might think that Frank would be embittered by this
but he simply said to Bert not to worry: he'd given his years
of labour completely willingly to see them both through
and he was glad he'd played his part in establishing
Bert's reputation. That was reward enough.

One day soon afterwards Bert came across Frank while Frank
was at his prayers and Bert almost wept to see his hands joined
in prayer – fine sensitive hands, spoiled by labour but somehow
having a glory of their own. And Bert made a sketch of them,
a sketch that still exists.

I've used the English versions of their names: Frank and Bert.
In fact they were German: Franz Knigstein and Albrecht Dürer.
The hands that had given everything to secure Albrecht's
future as an artist are perhaps the most loved hands in the
whole history of art: Albrecht Dürer's portrait of his generous
friend's Praying Hands.

Chapter 10

God has given the first place to Apostles.

Why do we have an extra feast for the conversion of St Paul –
but no extra feast for Peter? Well, you see, recruiting Peter
was fairly easy. Jesus walked down to the lakeside and there
were the fishermen, Simon and Andrew, mending their nets,
and Jesus asked them to become fishers of men. And they did.

But Saul of Tarsus was – if you'll forgive the expression –
a different kettle of fish altogether. Saul thought he knew it all.
He'd studied the scriptures and he prayed regularly in the synagogue
so he knew what was right and he was very irritated
by the followers of Jesus because they weren't getting it right.
And so when the leaders of the Jews began clobbering them,
Saul thoroughly approved. When they stoned Stephen to death,
Saul was there egging them on. The Lord had a big struggle
with Saul. He had literally to knock him off his horse on
the road to Damascus, and blind him to enable him to see.

Recruiting Saul, and turning him into Paul the apostle wasn't
an invitation; it was a miracle. But as we know, that conversion
turned Saul the Persecutor into Paul the Preacher.

Peter and Paul are the great apostles we reverence –
we give them first place among the saints.
And they remind me very much of ourselves.

Simon-Peter was easily recruited but lost heart
when the going got rough and ratted on Jesus.
He was not there standing alongside Mary and John
at the foot of the cross.

Saul was hostile to the Gospel – he was a bigot who thought he
knew all the answers and had to be brought down by God himself.

The history of the Church is full of people like that –
on one hand, people who practice the faith when it's
easy going, like Peter, and on the other hand people
who practice the faith because they think it endorses
their own prejudices, like Paul. And both those sorts
of people are missing the point of the Gospel. The faith
isn't about coasting along being goody-good, and it
isn't about condemning other people from the vantage
point of our own bigotry. The faith is what Peter and
Paul discovered it to be: it's about poor sinners like us,
deserving to die but being rescued by a Love so vast
that it eclipses all else. It's about a Saviour who found
us so useless that he had to die on the Cross for us.
It's about a Redeemer who rose from the dead in order
to prove that death is not the final end of life. It's about
giving us the hope and the courage to live life energetically
and whole-heartedly, not bogged down in peccadilloes
but opening our hearts to a life of love and generosity.
It's about seeing death as simply the passageway
into eternal peace with Christ.
Simon and Saul, Peter and Paul – and the other apostles too –
came through their cowardice and their bigotry and learned
from Jesus how to love. They loved Him so much they died
for Him. They loved us so much that they are praying for
us still. In the history of the Church God didn't give
priority to the pharisees who thought they knew everything.
He gave priority to apostles who discovered they knew
nothing and yet were called to discover eternal life with Him.

In the Church of today, as in all ages, there are Simons
who are full of enthusiasm when it's OK to be Catholic
and there are Sauls who are full of prejudices
and want to stone dissidents to death.
We all have within us the Simon and the Saul.
Let's beg God to transform us into Peters and Pauls.

Sir Thomas White, Merchant Taylor, was Lord Mayor of London in 1553. In 1555 he obtained a royal licence to found the College of St John the Baptist in Oxford. When he died in 1567 his body was buried in the college Chapel and one of the fellows, Edmund Campion, then still an Anglican, delivered the funeral oration. On Michaelmas 2003 Fr Cormac, a former Sir Thomas White scholar and later Merchant Taylors' Senior Scholar, offered Mass for his benefactor in the college chapel.

The original of this portrait hangs in the President's Lodgings and is reproduced here with the permission of the President and Fellows of St John's.

Chapter 11

So it was that John the Baptist appeared in the wilderness.

The English phrase 'tailor-made' implies very high professional skills.
Most of the things we buy are 'off the peg', but when
we want to look really elegant, then we need the 'bespoke',
tailor-made, specially for us. English tailoring has always had
a high reputation and it's no surprise that one of the City of London's
great livery companies is the Merchant Taylors.

I must declare an interest. Among the charitable activities of
the Merchant Taylors' Company is their school at Sandy Lodge.
I was a boy there for eight years and benefited greatly from
the excellence of the school.

Running a school was part of their brief.
The leading characteristics of the City of London livery companies
when they were founded were benevolence, religion and hospitality.
The Merchant Taylors' Company was founded in honour of
St John the Baptist and their school was founded in 1561
"in honour of Christ Jesus". Six years before the school was set up,
a leading Merchant Taylor, Sir Thomas White, founded a new
College in Oxford. He used the remains of an old Cistercian
house of studies, St Bernard's. and dedicated the new college
to the patron of the Merchant Taylors, John the Baptist.

I've always found it intriguing that the Merchant Taylors
chose *him,* of all saints, as their patron. Their whole wealth
and trade depended on dedication to fine clothes –
and their patron was the worst-dressed saint in heaven.
We heard in the Gospel that John had gone out
into the wilderness to seek spiritual inspiration.
He lived on locusts and wild honey and he wore
a garment of rough camel skin – hardly tailor-made.

But I know why the Taylors chose him as their patron.
In their Christian wisdom they saw clearly that clothes
do not make the man and that the saint of the wilderness
was a corrective and a warning.

For myself, I've always had a sneaky regard for people who
don't give a fig for their appearance. I remember one of
the masters at school with leather patches on the elbows of
his tweed jacket – always neat and clean, but his clothes
always looked very well worn. In those days, of course,
clothes had to last. They'd only just finished clothes rationing.
My childhood was a time of mending and patching,
of heeling and soling, of turning and darning.
Even now I tend to wear clothes until they fall apart.
Maybe it's the John the Baptist in me.

But don't get me wrong. I'm not knocking smartness and
appropriate dress. Clothes do matter. Remember the story
told by Jesus of the man who couldn't be bothered to dress properly
for a wedding and was punished for his lack of politeness.
Dressing appropriately is an aspect of courtesy,
and courtesy is an aspect of love. The Merchant Taylors
could dress up on ceremonial occasions with the best of
them. But there is a Christian awareness that noble robes
are no guarantee of a noble character.

The saint who most clearly proclaimed that was Francis of Assisi.
His rich father was in the rag trade, but Francis fiercely reacted
against the expense of fine cloth, not only because the poor
couldn't afford it, but because those who worked on dyeing the cloth
to create all those shimmering colours, often suffered terribly
from chemical reactions.

When the Taylors chose the saint of the wilderness, the
prophet in the camel–skin coat, as their role model, they
were reminding themselves of a different set of values,
a Franciscan set of values.

I readily concede that costume can often be an art form
in its own right. I love to admire fine fabrics.
I love to see elegant clothes on beautiful bodies;
I love to see impressive robes on state occasions;
But beware! I have to remember that remark by Jesus
that it is harder for a rich man to get to heaven
than for a camel to pass through the eye of a needle.

Beauty is of God, but if man values beauty of things
more than beauty of spirit he loses sight of God.
John's message from the wilderness was to look
beyond the obvious, to go beyond worldly values.

If we value human beings as fashion plates, we are deluded.
There are many wolves in well-tailored lambswool sweaters.
There are many villains in bespoke suits.
There are many harlots in couturier dresses.
Such people may be said to 'dress to kill'.
How's that for a great moral phrase: 'dressed to kill.'

If we dress up out of respect for the person we are with,
or to suit a particular occasion, fine.
But if we let appearance distort our values
we dress to kill – and it is our spiritual lives we kill.
Think of John the Baptist in his camel-skin.
Think of Herod in his royal robes.
Herod dressed to kill John the Baptist
for the flimsiest of reasons.

The question for us is simple: are our values those of John?
or Herod? The Merchant Taylors recognised that choice.
They accumulated wealth from fine clothes but they used
that wealth for wise purposes, and they deliberately held
in front of their eyes the image of a saint who didn't
give a fig for appearances.

And that, I think, is a strategy greatly to be commended.

In 1950, Fr Cormac's grandmother, Alderman Ellen McCormack, became Mayor of St Helens, in Lancashire.

Photo by Cholerton, St Helens

Chapter 12

Magnificat anima mea Dominum.

Anything with 'fifty' in it is a golden occasion. When I started
thinking about today's Golden Jubilee celebrations for Sister Nilda,
Sister Mary Carmel and Sister Ann, my mind went back to 1950 –
a year of Jubilee, a Holy Year – just a couple of years after
the launch of their life as religious.

In that Holy Year, my Grandmother became Mayor of St Helens
in Lancashire. It was the culmination of years of service
to the people of the town especially in relation to housing.
And it was thought very appropriate that Alderman McCormack
should be mayor in Holy Year because St Helens often claimed
to be the most Catholic town in England.

On mayor-making day the grown-ups had their official 'do' in
the Town Hall, but Granny Mac's grandchildren, myself included,
had something lighter in the Mayor's Parlour.
And afterwards we were given a tour of the Town Hall.

There, in the Council Chamber, was the large painting of the town's
patron, St Helen, mother of the Emperor Constantine and,
according to tradition, discoverer of the True Cross.
She was both as beautiful and as regal as imperial saints ought to be,
and she was holding the cross which she had unearthed from
its long hiding place. I remember the Latin motto:
Ex terra lux. From out of the earth light. It was a sort of
punning motto relating to all the collieries in the area –
out of the earth came light and heat.

Coal after all is only wood which has been buried for thousands
of years, rather than the few decades during which the Cross
of Christ lay hidden.

St Helen discovered it more or less in its entirety,
but of course that didn't last long – everyone wanted a piece of it,
and the wood on which Our Lord died
was splintered into millions of souvenirs.

It would be very easy to mock at that blend of piety and greed
which, by the time of the Reformation more than a thousand
years later, led to accusations that all the splinters, if gathered
together, would add up to several crosses. That may or may
not be true – it doesn't actually matter very much.
What *does* matter is the symbol of that splintered Cross.
Because, just as we are all members of Christ's body,
so we are all splinters of Christ's Cross.

There is in each and every one of us the need to be redeemed.
Christ hung on the Cross and that cross was formed
by the need to be redeemed. Between the two thieves,
justly executed, 'the midmost hangs for love'.
And the cross is therefore transfigured from a sign of disgrace
to the sign of overwhelming forgiveness; in this sign,
he has conquered. "Thou, thou, my Jesus,
after me didst reach thine arms out dying."

Nailed by history to the cross of our need for forgiveness,
Our Lord and Our God gave up life itself for us, and turned
darkness over all the earth into the glory of Easter morning;
his love fragmented to be enough for every one of us, his
cross splintered to serve as a symbol for all. The wonderful
thing is that in due course all that is fragmented and splintered
comes together in Him. That indeed was God's purpose
which he set forth in Christ, as a plan for the fullness of time,
to unite all things in Him.

Every soul that can stand *iuxta crucem,* beside the cross,
alongside Mary and the disciple he loved, every soul that can
gaze up at the Saviour as he breathes his last, every human
heart that can compassionate his Saviour thus cruelly treated,

every one of us who can place ourselves on Calvary becomes
a splinter of the True Cross – part of the tree on which he was
sacrificed – part of the cause of his agony.

But – and this is the glory of it – we do not end as dead splinters
of wood but transfigured, animated, rather as the spirit breathed
life through Ezekiel's Valley of dry bones and brought them to life.
We see ourselves no longer as dead splinters but as living parts of
the Mystical Body of Christ. St Helen triggered new devotion
to the most potent symbol of the overwhelming Love of God,
who felt it necessary to come among us and to share
our suffering and death so that we could share his eternal life.

There were many words bandied about on Calvary – orders,
obscenities. taunts and rebukes; but there were very few words
from the Cross. Love needs few words: "the love of my Lord
is the essence of all that I love here on earth. All the beauty
I see He has given to me and his giving is gentle as silence."
(Estelle White). It is the silent sacrifice which says everything.

As we survey that wondrous Cross the words of the bicentennial
Constitution of this order ring clearly in our ears. It is the vocation
of these jubilarians and all their sisters: "to understand
and to proclaim to others that the love of God has been revealed
to us in the most striking way in the passion and death of Jesus."

The Daughters of the Cross, contemplating Jesus, and his humility,
understand that they have to find him firstly in the Eucharist, and
then in the weakest and most suffering of his members.
In the life of the spirit nurtured in prayer,
in the work of life dedicated to making love incarnate,
we see that wonderful 'availability' which should characterise
the Daughters of the Cross, availability to the least of these
brethren of mine, the sick, the old, the helpless, the young,
the deprived, the handicapped. That awareness of Christ,
sacramentally present in the Eucharist and really present
too in the neediest of his members, is translated from awareness

into action by the consecration to community life.

I love the paragraph in the Constitution (28) which affirms the purpose of this vocation: "Where love reigns in a community the bonds that unite us to Christ are more easily maintained in all their strength and delicacy." Yes, that is Christlike; that is Mary: the perfect balance of strength and delicacy, the strength to pull down princes from their thrones, the delicacy to fill the hungry with good things.

Those familiar phrases come from Mary: they're part of the exultant song which broke forth from her when the infant John the Baptist leapt for joy at her approach, when she intuitively understood what it was that God wanted from her. Strength and delicacy: the bonds that unite us to Christ. It is no accident that two of the greatest paeans of faith in Christian worship express an outburst of scarcely containable joy.

Who would have thought that in a religion centred on a Cross, the most powerful response of humanity is joy unbounded! *Exultet. Magnificat.* At the Easter Vigil we rejoice in the light "which shines on in the dark and the darkness has never quenched it." "The power of this holy night dispels all evil, washes guilt away, restores lost innocence, brings mourners joy; it casts out hatred, brings us peace and humbles earthly pride." Joy unbounded. And in the *Magnificat,* Mary *exults* in God her Saviour, "Christ Jesus, our Lord, her God and her Son."

Three Daughters of the Cross exult today in five decades of response to the grace of their vocation, five decades of 'availability'. There are many people today with typing skills that they owe to Sr Ann, and there is the bedrock of her work as sacristan beneath this celebration today. There are many people today, especially in Ireland, who have suffered the unseen and unappreciated frustrations of deafness and who owe so much to the work of Sister Mary Carmel. There are many elderly ladies today who have the security of being in the safe hands of Sister Nilda – and I should add that if this homily has shown signs of having benefitted from the perceived necessity "of reading, meditating and immersing oneself in the Scriptures," then that is her doing too.

It is good that the *Magnificat* is the Gospel of this Mass. "It is the Lord who has done these great things . . . Holy is his name . . . he has come to the help of his servants."

Magnificat. Tell out my soul the greatness of the Lord.

Each of them has been called by name to help form this Institute, "so that his power may triumph over our weakness and so that wherever we go we may bring forth fruit, fruit that will last."

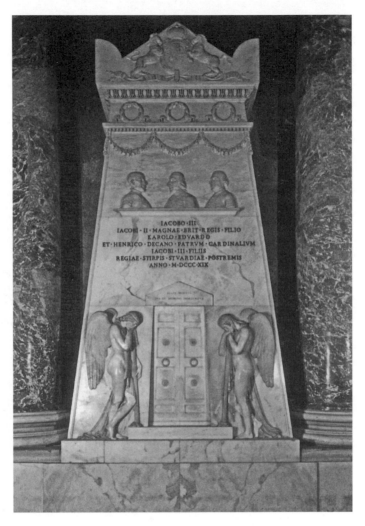

The Stuart Memorial in St Peter's Rome.

Canova's beautiful monument to "James III" and his two sons, Bonnie Prince Charlie and Cardinal York marks the end of the Stuart line of British Kings.

Henry Benedict, Cardinal York, 1725–1807. Ordained priest and Bishop of Ostia. Given the Red Hat 1747. In 1761 Bishop of Tusculum, living at Frascati. After the death in exile of Pope Pius VI, Cardinal York presided over the conclave, held in Venice, which elected Pius VII. When he died, he bequeathed the crown jewels, taken into exile by James II, to King George IV.

Chapter 13

Then he will take his seat on his throne of glory.

Most schoolboys know about Henry VIII and his six wives.
But who was Henry IX? He certainly existed.
In 1688 the last Catholic King of England,
James II – who was also James VII of Scotland –
went into exile. He thought that he was making
a tactical withdrawal, but his departure was interpreted
by his victorious opponents as an abdication.

His daughter Mary and her husband William of Orange
were crowned in his place; and after them his younger
daughter, Anne. But the exiled James also had a son –
another James, known to history as The Old Pretender,
because when the old king died, the son claimed to be
the rightful King of England.

Never once did he succeed in returning to England:
he spent his whole life in exile. And he had two sons:
Charles Edward and Henry Benedict. In 1745 Prince
Charles Edward made the final attempt by the exiled
House of Stuart to make a come-back. He became
known as 'Bonnie Prince Charlie.' But the attempt
failed and eventually Prince Charles died in Rome
a rather pathetic, lonely, old drunk.

The claim to be the rightful hereditary King of England
passed to his brother, the Duke of York, Henry, and he
was not only a Catholic priest but a Cardinal. He was
known as Henry Benedict, Cardinal York.

In the Vatican, Cardinal York was an important figure.
But the German Georges who occupied the throne of
England took no notice of him. They could see he would

never lead an invasion to get himself restored to the throne, and was no threat to them.

Henry, if he had been king, would have been Henry IX. And so he had some medals struck in Rome on which he described himself as

> *Henry IX, King, by the grace of God*
> *but not by the will of men.*

Interesting!

We tend to think that the crown passes automatically from father to son. The King is dead; long live the King. When George VI died in 1952, his daughter Elizabeth succeeded, our present Queen, and when she dies, the Prince of Wales will – as things stand – succeed her. But that hereditary process is something that evolved relatively recently. Centuries ago, it was by no means certain that a son would follow his father, or a sister follow her brother. What really mattered wasn't the hereditary right of succession but acceptance by the people.

A king was originally a man recognised by people as their best leader. Kings were chosen for their bravery and courage, good fighters rather than politicians. King Arthur, King Alfred, back in the mists of time. The High Kings of Ireland, like my namesake King Cormac of Cashel, were natural leaders chosen and accepted by the people.

It was only much later that kings tried to claim that they had a divine right to rule, as if the anointing at their coronation was a sign from God. But that was the high watermark of kingly ambition. A king can really only be king if the people want him to wear the crown. James II was king, but the country booted him out. The German Georges were imported to keep England Protestant. Bonnie Prince Charlie

failed to make a comeback and Henry, Cardinal York
summed it up very crisply: Henry IX, King, by the
grace of God but not by the will of men.

It is not a crown which makes a king but the loyalty
of his subjects. It is not inheritance which makes
a king, but acceptance.

And so it is with Christ.
Today we celebrate Christ the King,
but he can't be a king unless we choose him as our King.
A king has to be chosen because he represents
all that is best in his people.
When we speak of Jesus as Christ the King
we are not imagining some pompous official,
some jack-in-office promoted because his ancestors
did well. We are recognising that a king is only a king
when he is enthroned in the hearts of his subjects.

'Thy kingdom come' – we say it every day.
But only we can make it happen.

The candidate for kingship stands there waiting for us
to recognise him. At the moment, he *is* wearing a crown,
but it is a crown of thorns. That is the grace of God.
For his kingdom to *come* that crown of thorns
must be replaced by a crown of glory,
and *that* is by the will of men.

Christ seeks our recognition, our acclamation;
and when he is enthroned in our hearts
then he is truly king.

King by the grace of God and by the will of men.

West Cork, where the waters of the Gulf Stream bring warmth to the shores of Ireland. From the wellsprings and the brooklets, the trout streams and the rivers, the water flows down to the sea, the perfect image of the living water of God's grace. Here the Eccles Hotel in Glengarriff looks out over the sheltered tranquillity of Bantry Bay. As it was when Fr Cormac first saw it fifty years ago.

Chapter 14

Tormented by thirst, the people cried against Moses.

When I was a lad, Saturday morning was the time for Confession.
I'd cycle down from Croxley Green to Rickmansworth – not on
the main road which even then was dangerous – but what
we used to call the country way. A rough road down through
the woods, above the canal, across a couple of bridges
over the railway, past Sansom's farm and down the long footpath
to cross the river and emerge alongside the allotments and
Joan of Arc's playing fields, and beside the old Picture House.
It was a good bike-ride, mostly downhill.

Going back, I was inclined to dawdle. You could never tell
how many would be at Confession so arrival time was very
approximate. I could always spend quite a lot of time
lingering on the wooden slatted bridge over the fast-flowing
river, watching it tumble over the stones, watching the side-pools
and the weird eddies. Occasionally upstream there'd be a heron.
Further beyond, I knew there was the Scotsbridge Mill and
the water-cress beds. But here at my feet was the hurrying
river Chess, sparkling and chattering, making the most beautiful
music as it cascaded over the rocks in its way.

And usually before I left it and went on back home I'd reach
down from the wooden bridge and let the cold torrent flow
over my hands till they tingled and scoop up a handful to quench
my thirst. When I see almost-hidden streams in the mountains
of Mayo, or the Cherwell loping past me in Oxford, I'm always
entranced just as I was all those Saturday mornings ago.

Nowadays it's smart to drink water. On the radio on Friday
was a sommelier in a New York restaurant who offered diners
a choice of four still or four sparkling waters, as seriously as

a wine waiter in Pall Mall advising on vintages. And it's
easy to believe how different water will taste because it *looks*
so different. The river Chess was clear and cold – but the water
of Lough Allen which drains down from Slieve an Ireann,
the mountain of iron, has a bronze sheen which glimmers
like gold when you run your hands through it. Water from
the tap is boring, but whenever you think of water in nature,
it's almost a living thing, almost animated in its eagerness
to refresh and vitalise everything along its path.

It reminds us of Jeremiah's description of the accursed man
who has put all his trust in man and relied on the passing things
of life and turned away from good-heartedness. He becomes
like the dry scrub in the wastelands, struggling to survive in
the parched places of the wilderness, desolate and uninhabited.
But then there is the blessed man who puts all his trust in the
Lord of life and who is like the tree growing on the river bank
which thrusts its roots to the stream as it bubbles past and
takes in its life-giving nourishment so that even in
the great heat of summer it feels no discomfort;
its leaves stay green; it survives and bears fruit.

That's us. The river of grace flows past from the mountains
of God and offers life to all who come to it. Some people
choose to set themselves alongside the river so that they
can always drink. Others, maybe less fortunate, more busy,
nonetheless know where the river is and, like my long-ago self,
cycle down once a week, refreshing the soul with the water
of forgiveness as enjoyably as refreshing oneself with
the cool water of the river Chess.

Grace is like water, beautiful in itself, beautiful in its effects
and we know where it springs from and where to find it.

All we have to do is believe as Moses believed
and strike the rock so that the water flows.
All we have to do is believe as Bernadette believed

and scoop out the earth in the grotto so that the water flows.
All we have to do is believe and the grace of God
flows to us in a life-enhancing stream.

There is no flood, no drowning the landscape –
the days of Noah's inundation will never be repeated.
But the water is there, for us to seek.

The grace of our baptism, flowing over our head
to wash away the curse of sin. The grace of reconciliation
that sparkles with honesty and refreshes the soul. The grace
of friendship and intimacy and communion with God
when we eat and drink salvation to ourselves. The grace
of freshening enthusiasm as confirmation allows new springs
of grace to well up in our souls. The grace of commitment
that keeps us refreshed even in the arid periods of priesthood
or marriage. There is such a variety of graces, still or sparkling,
according to our needs.

And when the fever of life is over and the streams have mingled
in the meeting of the waters, one sees how full is that
great reservoir of grace, to see us through when peace
comes dropping slow.

    I will arise and go now, for always night and day,
    I hear lake water lapping with low sounds by the shore.

From the wellsprings and the brooklets, through the burns
and rivulets to the river and the fullness of the lake, the
living water of God's grace – sustaining and refreshing –
is ours for the taking through the sacraments.

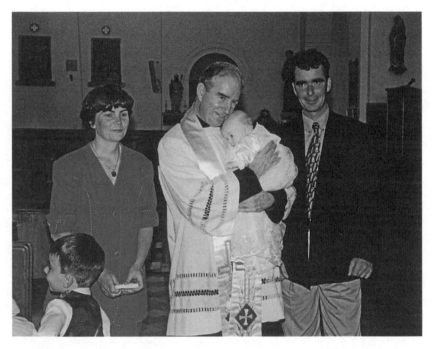

"One of the real joys of my life as a priest is baptising babies."

Fr Cormac holds Patrice Clare O'Reilly after her baptism at Most Sacred Heart, Ruislip in August 1994 with her parents Michael and Cathy and brother Liam.

Chapter 15

Simeon blessed them.

One of the real joys of my life as a priest is baptising babies.
Such a sense of wonderment surrounds a new baby,
and I find it deeply moving to share for a few moments
that wondering curiosity and optimism about the future.

The ups and downs of pregnancy are almost forgotten:
the morning sickness and the weird fluctuations in the
normal bodily chemistry; the scans that have shown
the wonderful growing underneath, the kickings that
speak of a different individual already living its own
life. Marriage had grown seamlessly out of courtship –
but pregnancy is the real life-changer. And then
the baby arrives and change becomes upheaval
and life is never the same again.

The baptism, the christening, is biblical in its impact.
The priest calls round to plan it, the choice of godparents
and readers, the candle and the white robe. And on the day
the parents and he are like Joseph and Mary and Simeon
squinting into the bright sunlight of the future and
wondering who this child will be. High hopes, of course,
and an awareness that there may be heartbreaks as well.

I'm not terribly keen on the practice of multiple baptisms.
I entirely see the logic of welcoming new members into the
worshipping community at a Sunday Mass and it is a nice *idea,*
but it doesn't seem to work well in practice: it tends to become
impersonal and to lose the all-important truth that each new
member is individually welcomed and uniquely loved. And it
loses the all-important sense of a baby at the heart of a *family.*

Every Sunday Mass is in one way or another a celebrating of community, the mystical body of Christ. But a baptism is special in another way: it is the equivalent of the presentation of Jesus in the temple; and there wasn't a normal Sabbath congregation for that: just the parents and baby Jesus, and they were welcomed to the temple by Simeon and Anna.

Baptism focuses on the individual: it bestows a unique Christian name to signify that the baby is uniquely loved by the God who has chosen this individual. And in my view that is best done in the context of family.

I love a baptism which gathers together the new baby's parents and their siblings and grandparents and cousins – and those close friends who are not blood relations but often turned into honorary aunties and uncles.

The mother and the father bring their baby into God's house to be identified and welcomed, to be anointed, to be planted and watered into the church. And I'm sure that like Mary and Joseph two thousand years ago they wonder what will happen: who will this child become?

I was baptised when I was a fortnight old on my father's birthday and I cherish the coincidence which I am sure was providential that many years later I was ordained on the forty-ninth anniversary of my baptism.

Dates are important in all our lives and I would always encourage parents to make a real fuss of three days every year, three days of special significance to each child.

The first one – and the one most generally observed – is the Birthday: the anniversary of emerging from the womb into independent life: that has to be an annual celebration, surely?

And then the Name Day – not celebrated as widely as I would like. I always encourage parents to identify a patron saint for their child, a saint who shares the same name. That Christian name deserves its own celebration. My birthday is in May but the feast of St Cormac is in September and I always feel a particular joy on that day, particularly because it also happens to be – providence again – the birthday of my best-loved friend. So the Name Day is the second great celebration.

And the third is the anniversary of the day when the child came into communion with the church: the anniversary of baptism. Celebrating that anniversary each year is a very good way of teaching the child about the real meaning of baptism.

In my guest-book at home one of my guests wrote that he had been particularly happy to have stayed in my flat on the anniversary of that day when he came into communion with his Christian host. It was the anniversary of baptism of Archbishop Derek Worlock and his guest-book entry prompted me to make much more of the anniversary of my own baptism so that, when years later – providence yet again – my ordination was fixed for my baptism anniversary, I saw a special blessing in that.

In any Catholic family, each member should celebrate all three dates: birthday, name day and baptism anniversary.

The most famous dirty feet in art belong to the
two pilgrims, and they are indeed very dirty.

Painting by Caravaggio in 1603-05

Chapter 16

They hustled him out of the town.

Sad, isn't it. Jesus of Nazareth returns to his home town
and goes to the synagogue where he'd worshipped as a boy.
But what he has to say sounds to them presumptuous, even
blasphemous. He says he's the fulfilment of the prophecy
of Isaiah and they're furious, and chuck him out.

Jesus of Nazareth has to take to the road and go elsewhere to
preach and teach. And I always imagine Jesus with dusty feet.
I was reminded of that when I was looking at the catalogue of
the exhibition at the Royal Academy – The Genius of Rome.
The culminating picture is by Caravaggio: Our Lady of Loreto.
It shows the Madonna at the door of her house with the infant
Jesus, no longer a baby, draped round her hip and reaching out
to a couple of pilgrims. The catalogue description caught
my eye: 'The most famous dirty feet in art belong to the two
pilgrims in Caravaggio's Madonna di Loreto' – and they are
indeed very dirty.

The story was that Mary's old home in Nazareth, where
her son was not honoured, was transported by angels to
Loreto in Italy. There the simple little carpenter's house
was encased in a sumptuous church and became a place
of pilgrimage. When the faithful reached Loreto they'd
circle the Holy House three times on their knees.

Caravaggio shows an elderly peasant couple kneeling at
their journey's end at the threshold of the Holy House, and
the Christ Child in Mary's arms reaches out to welcome
and bless them. The couple have their backs to us as they
kneel to Our Lady and you can't help but notice the wear
and tear on the poor old fellow's feet.

71

It set me thinking about pilgrim journeys.

Many years ago, my Mother and I, and an aunt, went on
a pilgrimage to Rome. We stayed at the Casa Pallotti
by the Ponte Sisto over the Tiber, a hostel much used by
pilgrims from Germany. And there we met a couple from
Bamberg who became very good friends. They came to
my ordination in 1988 and Elizabeth makes up a special
calendar for me each year. This year her theme was
experiencing the Spirit in different holy places.
She and her husband Karl are incredible travellers –
like the pilgrims of old. Not tourists, but pilgrims in quest
of holy places.

So January shows Rome where we first met as pilgrims.
February sees the feast of Our Lady of Lourdes and she has
cut out an invitation to the diocese of Westminster in 1990 –
Cardinal Basil Hume inviting his people to join him on a
pilgrimage to Lourdes. March is Patrick's month and the
pilgrim place is Lough Derg where my mother used to go.
June takes us to St Anthony's shrine in Padua, August to the
Black Madonna of Czestochowa in Poland, September to
Cormac's chapel on the Rock of Cashel, October to Assisi,
and so on.

God is everywhere of course, and in that sense he is as close to
us at home as anywhere else. Of course. But there are places
hallowed by association, blessed with a special aura by the
holiness of our ancestors, and we gain strength by following
in their footsteps. I have been inspired myself in Lourdes by
the quiet triumph of love over commercialism. And beneath
the baroque splendour of St Peter's in Rome I remember the
awareness of holiness I felt as a pilgrim praying at the tomb
of Pius XII.

In a funny way the more home means to us, the more we need
to be pilgrims. I am by temperament a home-builder and

I perceive the need to go beyond the home, the cocoon,
the oasis, and to seek the holy places of my own life.
I go to Blenheim where I began to understand love
and I go to Lough Allen where my grandfather and my mother
anchored their faith. Such pilgrimages are highly personal.

But there's also the element of travelling with others
linked by a common purpose. And sometimes coming across
an unexpected fellow traveller.

Like the two disciples who fled from Jerusalem after the Crucifixion
and walked to Emmaus and whose mysterious companion
on the road they recognised at the breaking of bread.
Like St Peter who was so disillusioned and dispirited by his
apparent failure in Rome that he set off to return to Galilee.
And he'd scarcely got beyond the City gates on to the Appian
Way when he saw the Lord, coming towards him and carrying
his Cross towards Rome.

Quo vadis, Domine? cried Peter. Where are you going, Lord?
And Jesus pointed to the road of destiny, the road to Rome.

There is a real sense in which we won't get to heaven in
carpet slippers. Pilgrims end up with very dirty feet.

It would be sentimental and attention-seeking if I were
to imitate my grandfather and walk to Mass barefoot –
and yet I know in my heart of hearts that the mental attitude
I must have all through life is not to be cosy,
but to see life as a pilgrimage
from holy place to holy place,
and to finish my journey with dusty feet.

The kingfisher, the halcyon, is the beautiful symbol of rare times of peace and tranquillity, especially in the season of mists and mellow fruitfulness. In Shakespeare's *Henry VI*, Joan of Arc promises a restoration of peace in France: "Expect Saint Martin's Summer, halcyon days, since I have entered into these wars."

On a visit to the Edinburgh Festival, Fr Cormac saw a beautiful enamel brooch of a kingfisher and brought it home as a present for his Mother. She loved it and after her death her son frequently wears it in his own lapel. This drawing of the brooch is by Jo Lamb.

Chapter 17

I want you to be happy, always happy in the Lord.

Sermon preached at the evening Mass when
Fr John Luke's body was brought into St Luke's,
Pinner, to rest there overnight before his
Requiem and burial, June 2003

I can never forget the first time that John invited me to join
him at the theatre in Stratford–upon–Avon. He had booked
tickets for the Swan for *The Country Wife* and we decided
we'd make a full day of it, and break our journey for
refreshment at my flat in North Oxford.
It was late September, a beautiful day, almost ten years ago,
and we went for a stroll down to the river Cherwell.
I love that quiet stretch of the riverbank where Moley and
Ratty first registered their presence with Kenneth Grahame.
And I love to observe all the other creatures that live
along its banks. I just happened to be looking downstream
and saw this tiny shape streaking towards us along
the centre of the river. We both watched as it approached
and flashed past us and disappeared.

It was the first time I'd seen a kingfisher on that particular
stretch of river, and the brilliance of that sapphire blue arrow
against the greens and russets of the leaves was startling
in its intensity. It was a moment of absolute magic,
and it seems absolutely right that an experience of colour
so startling and so memorable should occur in John's company.

I cherish such 'kingfisher moments' – but they are rare.
Sometimes they are visual. John was wonderfully aware
of colour and the texture of fabrics and the effectiveness

of set designs and the potency of lighting and it showed
in his approach to church furnishings and vestments.

Sometimes these memorable moments came from wonderful
actors: Toby Stephens as Coriolanus, Jane Lapotaire as
Catherine of Aragon, Judi Dench as Filumena — all of these
I shared with John. But I suspect that most of his 'kingfisher
moments' were musical. He had a most perceptive ear,
whether it was for the delicacy of Purcell, or Schubert,
or Mozart or for the power of Verdi and Tchaikovsky.

There is always a danger of course, that such pleasures
can remove people from reality into a remote and rather selfish
clique. But John's musical 'kingfisher moments' all fed back
into his life and his vocation. The concerts here in this church
delighted and thrilled him — and many other people besides.
And he always shared his pleasure with great generosity.

Gerard Manley Hopkins had a similar intensity of response to
the beauty of the natural world and the glories of God's creation.
He clearly felt a scruple about loving them so much and he asked
himself the forthright question: "To what serves mortal beauty?"
He answered it honestly: "See, it does this: keeps warm
men's wits to the things that are — what good means."

John had examined his conscience in a similar way.
He cherished the gifts God gave him, and he delighted
in the 'kingfisher moments' of vision and perception which
open our minds and hearts to the beauty deep down things
and to 'God's better beauty, grace.' John's aesthetic alertness
enriched his priesthood and stimulated his great gift for friendship.
He was the most hospitable and generous of friends.

One of his strategies was the nice meal out — but another,
just as frequent and just as enjoyable, was lunch at home —
very simple, just the two of us. I was in awe of his cooking,
but the meal was incidental: it was the conversation
that mattered.

He was a shrewd observer of human foibles
and his natural inclination was to believe the best of people,
and that could occasionally result in disillusionment.
But his natural cheerfulness was uppermost –
he had a merry sense of mischief and he wasn't one
to nurse resentments.

All that really matters is to live in the presence of the Lord.
He was both gentle and forthright, a good combination
in a priest. His interest in people was not a professional pose;
he was a natural listener and people appreciated that.
He was quick to recognise the gifts of others and respectful
of different viewpoints. He was quite happy to disagree
with someone, but it never occurred to him that opposition
to a way of doing things could mean hostility to the person.
"What do *you* think?" was a phrase often on his lips.
He was a civilised man who expected a civilised response
and was only rarely disappointed.

Above all he was a happy man who took genuine pleasure
in making others happy. It's easy to hear John's voice echoing
those words of St Paul: "I want you to be happy, always happy
in the Lord. I repeat, what I want is your happiness."
And immediately after happiness, in Paul's book, comes
tolerance. That's not to say that John couldn't be off-hand
and terse when people were careless. Argue a different view
from his and he'd have no problem, but fail to honour a
commitment and he'd get very cross – he lived an ordered life
himself and didn't appreciate disorder in others.

But tolerance was actually his strong suit.
His ecumenical achievements were considerable.
They sprang from his own deep tolerance
and from his respect for the history of others.
He was himself deeply happy in the Catholic Church
and as a priest, but he never ceased to love and respect

his own roots, and he never forgot the common ground
shared by those who are God's friends, not least
God's chosen people. He rarely missed a meeting
that might help to bring people together.

He was able to do a lot in his eighteen years in Pinner,
building on established traditions and working quietly
and conscientiously to maintain the vitality of the parish.
Eventually, going past the three-score-years-and-ten milepost,
he had to recognise that he hadn't as much energy
as he felt necessary to do the job properly. And so he retired.
It's almost exactly a year now since he came back
to St Luke's for his official farewell. And I think
that was a 'kingfisher moment' for him: an evening
of warmth and affection which eased the pain
of his having to leave. He stayed with me
in Stanmore that night after the party,
and it was good to see him so truly happy.

Down at Ditchling he enjoyed the friendliness
of nearby clergy and was very happy to help out
by saying Masses. He had walked to Emmaus
and he had identified the Lord in the Eucharist,
and that was not just a belief: it was an enthusiasm.

I'm sure he'd have been very content with the hymn
that escorted him back into his church tonight:

Richer than gold is the love of my Lord,
better than splendour and wealth.

And he'd be saying to all of us who are grieving
at the suddenness of his death: No need to worry –
but if there's anything you need, pray for it, thankfully.

"Rejoice in the Lord alway."

He has been a good friend to many of us. And I'm sure
there have been many of those 'kingfisher moments'

when God's creation can be appreciated in all its beauty,
and when the immortal diamond in each of us
becomes suddenly and wonderfully apparent.

Finally, says Paul; finally, says John:
fill your minds with everything that is true,
everything that is noble, everything that is good and pure,
everything that we love and honour, and
everything that can be thought virtuous or worthy of praise.
Keep doing all the things that you learnt from me. . .
then the God of peace will be with you.

"Farewell, but not for ever, brother dear."

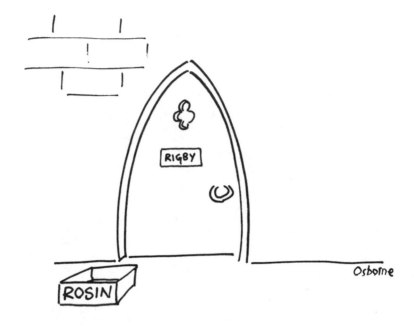

When Fr Cormac left Radio 3 in 1985, he received many letters of good wishes, especially from ballet-lovers who remembered *Royal Repertoire*, his series reflecting the music used by the Royal Ballet companies during the 1970s. The rosin box that stands in the wings so that dancers can protect themselves from slipping was translated by one well-wisher into a seminary situation! Fr Cormac framed the cartoon. Twenty years on, he was concelebrant at a Mass in St Anselm & St Cecilia at which his friend David Titterington was being received into the Church, and was amazed to discover that the person serving the Mass was no other than Stephen Osborne who had sent him the cartoon in 1985. Permission was immediately sought and granted, to reproduce the cartoon in this third collection of sermons.

Chapter 18

The one who enters through the gate is the shepherd.
Anyone who gets in some other way is a thief and a brigand.

Whenever we are asked to think about priesthood
I think back to the good priests who were my role models.

I remember going down to Rickmansworth,
sitting in the shade under the trees,
behind the great open-air crucifix
in the presbytery grounds.
An Assumptionist parish.
Fr Walter was drilling aspiring seven-year-olds
to become altar boys:

> *Introibo ad altare Dei.*
> *Ad Deum, qui laetificat juventutem meam.*

Then when Croxley was hived off and became a separate parish,
our first Parish Priest was Mgr Clarke,
a lovely ex-army chaplain with a hacking smokers' cough
and jumbo ears. It was an inspiration to watch him
saying Mass because he clearly loved it so totally.

At university, a calm and persuasive Belgian, Père Yves,
an intellectual who later became a Dominican,
rigorous but perceptive.

And Fr Michael Hollings, a true saint,
a man capable of both trenchant rebukes
and kindly understanding, above all a man of thoughtful prayer
who seemed to have humanity in proportion
as he held the Almighty in his heart.

And during my first abortive attempt to be a priest in Rome,
the quiet but steely Monsignor Worlock,

determined to make justice and peace
the watchwords of church influence.

Five priests – so utterly different in style, but all of them with
a clear sense of purpose, and therefore profoundly inspiring.
They wanted – all of them – to centre their whole lives
on the Mass. They were interested, and involved, in all sorts
of aspects of church life but each one of them felt himself
a true priest at the altar, offering the sacrifice of the Mass.

And that was true also of three long-dead priest-heroes
of Oxford whose lives and writings were a major influence.
Edmund Campion, founder-member of St John's, my own
College; scholar, Jesuit, martyr.
John Henry Newman, Trinity and Oriel, writer,
preacher and Cardinal;
and Gerard Manley Hopkins, of Balliol, Jesuit and poet.
All of them ready to make any personal sacrifice
to offer the sacrifice of the Mass.
It was what they *did,* because they were priests,
that underpinned their spiritual lives.

And that explains why I was so surprised to read Cardinal
Murphy–O'Connor's pastoral letter which is printed in full
in the newsletter this week. He describes how he used to ask
young men just arriving at the seminary in Rome why they
wished to be priests. Few, he says, could reply very precisely.
They were more concerned with what they wanted to be: priests,
than with what they wanted to do as priests.
Maybe that's what's gone so terribly wrong with the Church
in recent years: a lack of clarity in priests
about what they ought to be doing.

It's not very convincing to say that a priest is a man of
understanding and sympathy – that surely is the vocation
of every Christian. Every single one of us has to have
the capacity to love and understand. The vocation to priesthood

goes beyond that – in a sense, takes that for granted.

If someone comes to me and says he wants to be a man of
understanding who has sympathy and can read human hearts,
I might well suggest he become a teacher, a doctor, a care worker –
or just an ordinary person in an ordinary job who uses his life
to bring God's love into the world around him
as a husband and father.

I would direct him towards priesthood ONLY
if to those highly desirable human ambitions of love
and service he could add an overwhelming desire
to be a channel of God's grace through the sacramental life
of the Church. Because *that* is what a priest *does*.

A priest makes it possible for the sacramental life of the Church
to exist, and if a seminarian does not come with that perception
I would think him better off elsewhere.

I would want to hear that the would-be priest
was already in love with Jesus in the Blessed Sacrament
and longed above all to say Mass and to carry the Sacrament
to the people of God.
Ego volo celebrare Missam. I wish to say Mass.

If there are young men – or indeed old men – who can say that
and who see no better way of living their lives,
the Church would be well served.

This is a time of crisis for the priesthood because
so much trust has been abused. The betrayal of vows
is always a shock – whether it is lay people
breaking their marriage vows and drifting into affairs
and adultery, or whether it is priests breaking their vow
of celibacy and drifting into hypocrisy
and child abuse.

What is shocking is that people have lost track
of what it is they are supposed to be *doing*.

They're so obsessed with *being* themselves,
expressing their own personalities,
that they lose contact with what they're supposed to *do*.

A married man subordinates being himself to being a loving
husband and a good father and sacrifices a lot of himself
to achieve that. In the same way a priest subordinates being
himself to being a celibate and a good shepherd and sacrifices
a lot of himself to achieve that. The present priority of 'being
myself', above being a husband or being a priest, is deeply
corrosive of vocation. We need more priests just as we need
more good husbands – men willing to sacrifice themselves
for those they love.

I can promise you it is not *more* difficult to be a good priest
than to be a good husband. They are both vocations and
both demand self-sacrifice. A man who doesn't understand
that shouldn't proceed to matrimony or holy orders.

The scandals of bishops who father children or of priests
who abuse children come as a terrible blow to us
because, like adultery, they are deeds of betrayal –
betrayal of trust, betrayal of vocation, betrayal of vows.

We need to pray for those who've lost their way
and for those who've been their victims;
and we need to pray for more and better priests.
Listening to me now is one person who is being asked by God
to do something special with his life.
It is a call which involves much sacrifice;
it is distinctly underpaid but I assure you
it is a most abundantly-rewarded career choice:
a decision to go beyond coming to Mass
and to be a bringer of the Mass to others.

A priest can be any sort of person.
It's what all these various types *do,* all of them, that matters.
What a priest *does* is to enable the grace of God
to flow through the sacramental life of the Church
to the people of God,
particularly in the Eucharist.
He centres his life on the Mass
every day of his priesthood
so that the people may be fed
with the daily bread, the Daily Bread,
for which Jesus taught us to pray,
the bread of life which *is* Jesus himself.

Chapter 19

This day new light will shine upon the earth.
The Lord is born for us.

A Christmas morning sermon, preached in
Cardinal Newman's Oratory at Littlemore, 2004

I had a surprise phone call yesterday afternoon, Christmas Eve,
from a priest in Tasmania. He'd already said his two Vigil Masses,
and was preparing for the Midnight – eleven hours ahead of ours.
But he made the time to give me a delightful present –
the knowledge of his thoughtfulness, his love
and his prayers.

We were laughing at the contrast between his Christmas
and mine, his hemisphere and mine. I was looking out at a
torrent of freezing rain. He was sweltering in his vestments.
Many of the traditional carols are sung down there too, but
such favourites as *In the Bleak Midwinter* don't actually
sound too relevant in Australia.

Mark said how odd it was, in a way, that they had before them
this northern hemisphere imagery
of the light shining through the darkness
when in fact the sun was beating down on them.

I am mindful of that contrast this morning. The dawning of
a new light seems very apt to us, whereas their skies are cloudless
and ablaze with light. But that should remind us of that first
Christmas when the natural darkness of the northern hemisphere
was suddenly replaced by a blazing in the heavens as potent
as an antipodean midsummer. It wasn't the light of the
Tasmanian sun but the glory of the Lord. Not the glare
of a midsummer day but the haloes of a host of angels.
What a message it conveys. The birth of a Saviour is not

a distant twinkling star, it's not the gentle silvery moon:
it is the blazing truth of God's love for mankind.

Ignem veni mittere in terram: I came to bring fire to the earth.
And that fire was not the wantonly destructive force
of a forest fire, but the Promethean fire
that could transform the lives of men:
the warming power of love.

When I heard Mark's voice coming so unexpectedly from
the other side of the world, the light of love burned brightly.
Cor ad cor loquitur: Heart speaks to heart –
nowhere better than Littlemore to savour those words.
Our task as we preach the Gospel is not to bombard the world
with words but to live the life of the Word of God,
to light the world with that goodness, that warmth,
that thoughtfulness, that love, one to one, *cor ad cor.*

Unsurprisingly the Church chooses as the Gospel for the main
morning Mass of Christmas the opening of John's Gospel.
John proclaimed that the life of the Word of God was
the light of men – a light that shines in the darkness.

The various translations of the passage have difficulty
in conveying the sheer magnitude and power of that light.

I quite like the precise academic phrase chosen by Lancelot
Andrewes and his colleagues: "And the light shines
in darkness; and the darkness comprehended it not."
The New Jerusalem prefers a rendering which suggests
a battle between opposing forces: "Light shines in darkness
and darkness could not overpower it."
But my favourite is the version in the New English Bible:

> The light shines on in the dark
> and the darkness
> has never quenched it.

There is such a sense of historical continuity in that –
the light shines on; the darkness has never quenched it.

The light is the life of love; God's love for his creation,
God's individual love for each one of his creatures.
God's love for the whole of his creation was always there,
but what Jesus became man to reveal, what we needed
to understand was that it was not remote love, not
love *de haut en bas*. It is one to one. It is *cor ad cor*.
It is the Sacred Heart of Jesus and the heart of me.

In Tasmania and in Oxford the message is very clear.
There are times when it is bleak midwinter and the speck
of light in the overshadowing darkness is the dawn of hope.
There are times when it is bright midsummer and the
vibrancy of Johannestag is the noon of faith.

And unifying the dawn of hope and the noon of faith
is the warmth of love, one-to-one love.

In both hemispheres there is the truth this Christmas
that when the angels gathered
to reflect love's loveliness
into the world below,
it is a new light that shines upon us,
the Lord who is born for us,
the light of God's redeeming love.

Chapter 20

Christ Jesus is the image of the unseen God.

When I was a child words came easily to me.
The cat sat on the mat; and I knew what a cat was.
Only later did I understand that *Puss in Boots* and
Magical Mr Mistoffelees and *The Lion King* are
much more complex characters than the word 'cat' signifies.
So I had to extend my vocabulary to explore the
amazing variety of feline mystery. There's more to cats
than Tom & Jerry.

But even the most extensive vocabulary has its limits.
How often do we experience feelings
that are far too deep for words.

A couple of months ago I was standing near Allihies on the
ring of Beara looking out across the Kenmare river estuary,
totally unable to find words for the feelings welling up in me.
It wasn't just the beauty of the sun glinting on the water or
the high-piled cloudscape above the blue mountains of Kerry.
It was also the exultant joy of being there against the odds,
and the surge of memories it evoked.   A feeling of
total immersion in delight. Words can't begin to express it.

The word love, like the word cat, is only the very first step
towards comprehending life's mystery. We realise very quickly
that words are inadequate.

Everything I love about Ireland and my mother and my faith
and my friendships and my priesthood suddenly became
apparent to me, looking across the Kenmare River that afternoon
– but I don't have the words or the time to pin it down.

All I could do was fill my lungs with that pure air and feel deep
within me the goodness of everything and everyone I love.
And to think "I love this, I believe in this:
it is good for me to be here."

The great Russian ballerina Anna Pavlova was once asked by
an admirer what she was trying to convey through her dancing.
Pavlova was puzzled. "Well", she said, "If I could *tell* you,
I wouldn't dance it."

So when we try to tell people about God, try to find words
to pin God down, we are almost doomed to disappointment.
'Immortal, invisible, God only wise' says the hymn-writer,
and somehow it's very remote and distant. We struggle to
hold eternity in a phrase; we call creation a Big Bang and
the sheer wonder of it eludes us.

> O Lord, my God, when I in awesome wonder,
> consider all the worlds thy hand has made,
> I see the stars, I hear the rolling thunder,
> thy power throughout the universe displayed.
> *(Stuart K Hine)*

Even that only begins to express the reality. And yet we need
to keep making the effort, to see beyond the humdrum
to the deep realities of our existence: our joy in living,
the magic of being in love, the dynamism of happiness,
the confidence in a vitality that is indestructible.

That almost wordless understanding of it is there in our souls.
And when I am lonely, or in pain, it's my soul that exults in
God my Saviour and keeps me close to those inexpressible realities.

Yes, at times, it seems almost too difficult.
God is beyond words; God is invisible; God is a mystery.
And all that is true. But we can still *know* God.
We can have that deep inner feeling of recognition
when we look across at him, just as I looked across to the hills,
and know and love everything about what we see.

Deep inside us, when words fail and love lies hidden,
we *know* what love *means*.

We fill our lungs with the spirit of the Lord and we feel
love of life, love of being alive, love of being part of creation,
love of the creator. In that way, we can truthfully say
>Yes – I know God
>
>>I worship God
>>
>>I thank God
>>
>>I love God

And in a very real sense the immensity of God is within us;
we can contain God in our hearts. He himself has made it possible
for us. He has no need of our love but he longs for our love.
And so he took an almost unimaginable step to enable us
to know him. He knows perfectly well that the human heart
cannot contain an infinity of love.

And so he came to share our experience.
In the fullness of time, the second person of the Trinity
became one of us.

Jesus is our Lord and our God, and our favourite brother;
he is infinite and eternal, and our closest friend.
He walks beside us; our hearts beat in harmony with his;
he shares his life with us. And all our frustration
with the inadequacy of words fades into insignificance.

I do not stand impotently in front of a remote deity.
I lean my head on the shoulder of the God
who is also the man I love.

The Jesus who lives and breathes in the four Gospels;
the Jesus who comes to me under the appearance
of bread and wine, this Jesus is the image of the unseen God
and we fill our lungs with the spirit of Our Lord.

Some musical friendships have been made since Fr Cormac's twenty years in the BBC. The great Czech organist–composer, Petr Eben, was due to perform his Comenius-inspired work *The Labyrinth of the World* in Westminster Cathedral. At short notice they were without a narrator, and Fr Cormac was asked to do it. It was a happy collaboration, so when later David Titterington gave a performance of this and other Eben pieces requiring a narrator, he too asked Fr Cormac. This photo was taken at Downside where Professor Titterington (right) was playing an Eben piece in the presence of the composer (left). Next to Fr Cormac is Graham Melville Mason, expert on Czech music and a former BBC colleague.

Chapter 21

They warned the apostles not to speak in the name of Jesus.

It follows, therefore, that we who are the heirs
of the apostles must *always* speak in the name of Jesus.
Indeed, every word we utter must reflect the spirit of Jesus.

This is not an invitation to lip-service: far from it.
It is the recognition that what fills our minds and hearts
will normally determine what we say and how we say it.

Let me digress. You know what it's like to have a tickle
in the throat. You're sitting there listening intently to
the sermon and suddenly you want to cough and you try
desperately to suppress it and swallow hard and stuff
a handkerchief in front of your mouth. And you nearly
choke in the attempt not to cough. Imagine what it's
like for me, up here, and suddenly I'm aware of phlegm
on my vocal chords and I desperately want to clear
my throat and I wish I had a 'cough key'.

In each news studio when I began my broadcasting life
the announcer had a cough key. If he needed to clear
his throat he pressed down the key which took him
off the air until he released it again, throat cleared.

It was very useful, the cough key. Though not always
used as intended. On one occasion the sub-editor handed
the newsreader a story about a major bank robbery and
the story ended with the pithy sentence: "After snatching
the bullion the robbers got away in a fast car." The newsreader
paused, pressed the cough key and said sarcastically to the sub:
"Well I hardly supposed that they used a slow one."
Unfortunately, that day the cough key was out of circuit and
so the comment was heard the length and breadth of Britain.

I was listening a few days ago to Radio 4's tribute programme
to Alistair Cooke. Some minutes into the programme
a woman's voice was superimposed talking loudly to a colleague
just going off duty. We heard a couple of minutes of domestic
bric-à-brac eclipsing poor Mr Cooke. I imagine that instead
of operating the talk-back key connecting the studio and
the control cubicle, the lady had pressed the wrong key and
accidentally put herself on air. God knows it's easy enough
to lose concentration.

And then last week we had the football commentator
who assumed he had come off air and made some offensively
racist comments about a footballer. And what a hoo-ha in
the tabloids. He resigned from his job and banished himself
from the pages of *The Guardian*.

Microphones – treacherous things: faders, talk-back facilities,
cough keys all give a false sense of security – but that's not
the problem. The problem was what was said.

We might think that it's tough luck that something not intended
for widespread distribution was broadcast by a technical error.
It is indeed tough luck. But it underlines the point that if
the words had been wise and sensible it wouldn't have mattered.

If the thoughts in our minds and the feelings in our hearts are
always free from contamination, it doesn't matter who hears us.
The only way to ensure that offensive words do not become
a problem is never to utter them. If we allow ourselves in
some imagined privacy to denigrate our brothers and sisters
in Christ, with harsh and offensive phrases, we are not speaking
in the name of Jesus.

Gertrude, you may remember, begged her son Hamlet to speak
to her no more: "These words like daggers enter in mine ears."
We have to be constantly aware that words have a cutting edge.
We ourselves, the Catholics of this country, have in the past
been the victims of such daggers. Our ancestors were attacked

with the word 'papists' or the derisory word 'rednecks', words coined in order to vilify. Such words of vilification should never be in our thoughts, let alone on our lips. They are daggers, weapons honed by hatred and they have no place in any Christian's vocabulary.

We need to examine our consciences and check our vocabulary – whether spoken or unspoken is neither here nor there – and to eradicate the dagger words. If we ever refer, even in our silent thoughts, to one of our brothers or sisters in Christ in the vocabulary of vilification we have a confession to make and work to do.

Papist, Prod, Nigger, Paki, Jewboy, Yid, Poofter, Queer – these are the daggers of mindless prejudice. We should never use such words. We should never think such thoughts. It's not to protect ourselves from being caught out by faulty technology. Faulty technology cannot betray us unless we have already betrayed Christian thinking.

We speak what is in our minds, we put into words what fills our hearts. And so we have to train our minds and hearts to think always the thoughts of Christ. There must be no verbal daggers if we speak in the name of Jesus.

Chapter 22

The beginning of the Good News
about Jesus Christ, the Son of God.
It is written in the book of the prophet Isaiah . . .

That's how today's Gospel started – it's the opening
of St Mark's Gospel, quoting the prophet Isaiah.
And we all listened very carefully, because it's all
in the good book, the Bible.

Why do we attach such importance to that book?
Why do we regard it as in some way inspired by God?

If you look at the table of contents at the beginning
of a bible, you'll see that more than two thirds of it
is a pull-together of miscellaneous Jewish literature
more than two thousand years old.

The remaining third is Christian: four Gospels, a sequel to
one of them (Luke) which we call the Acts of the Apostles;
and a weird selection of teaching letters from apostolic times.
The question I want to ask when I see a book like that is,
who edited it?

I can see that it's by all sorts of different authors:
some historians, some poets, some prophets, biographers,
and theologians. But who pulled it all together
and decided what would go into it and what would
be left out? Who was the compiler? Who was the editor?

People often say that the Bible has all the answers –
but who gave us the Bible? If what looks like a very
random selection of ancient texts is going to be set up
as some sort of Holy Book; I want to know who it was
who had the clout to decide that the Gospel of Mark
was inspired and that other Gospels were not.

I want to know why a letter to the Hebrews was included,
even though no-one knows who wrote it; but a letter from
St Clement was omitted. How can you have an inspired
letter written by Anon? Who put this lot together
and identified it as the Word of God?

For the first few centuries of the Christian era there wasn't
a Bible. The synagogues of the Jews held hundreds of
scrolls of the Hebrew testament, but the Christians had
nothing comparable for many years.

When the first Eucharists were celebrated there were no
readings from the Gospels because they hadn't been written.
Before the Gospels came to be written, the first Christian
teachings to be put on paper were in the letters which Paul and
others wrote to their recent converts to encourage their faith.
Converts in Corinth, and Rome, and Philippi. And others,
hearing about those letters, copied them and read them aloud
at Mass just as we do now.

It wasn't until Peter died in Rome during the great persecution
of Nero in 64 AD that they saw the urgent need to put down
on paper all the things Peter had told them about Jesus.
Before Peter died, the stories of Jesus had been told and retold.
When he was put to death, the Christians in Rome almost
certainly got his young friend Mark to write down all that
he could remember from what Peter had told them.
Mark was probably the first, then later Matthew and Luke,
and eventually John.

By the year 200, the Christian churches had all sorts of scrolls;
they were awash with Gospels and letters. Each community
had its own treasures and circulated copies to others.
By the second half of the fourth century it was pretty chaotic.
Lots of good stuff – and lots of rather dubious stuff.
All very edifying – but was it reliable?

There was for example a letter from Peter that had survived.

Another, claiming to be from him, was good stuff too.
But not by Peter. There was an Apocalypse of Peter
and the Acts of Peter and even a Gospel of Peter.
And you won't find any of these in the Bible today.
Why not? Who decided not to include them?

The man we really ought to thank was one of Peter's successors as
leader of the Church in Rome. He was elected in October 366
and was Bishop of Rome for eighteen years. His name was
Damasus, and for many years he employed as his secretary
the great scholar, St Jerome. Pope Damasus got Jerome to revise
the various versions of the Gospels, and by 382 the Pope felt able
to promulgate some sort of reliable Christian New Testament
to go alongside the well-established Hebrew Testament of the Jews.
Jerome's work gave us, for the first time, a recognisable
canon of scripture. Although the letters had been written first,
it made more sense to put the Lives of Jesus first. So in Jerome's
Vulgate, the Christian Testament starts with Matthew, Mark,
Luke and John.

When you hear it said that Christians don't need a church
and they don't need a Pope because all they need is the scriptures,
just ask where they think the Bible came from.
Who edited it? Who decided what was inspired and what wasn't?
And remember St Damasus, whose feast we celebrate on 4 December.

All those sources sorted, edited, translated.
All those ingredients studied and sifted.
All those writings investigated and given to Jerome
to translate into good Latin that everyone could understand.

It was the authority of Damasus as Bishop of Rome
that enabled him to say: "This is the Word of the Lord."
Let us, on this Bible Sunday, thank God for St Damasus,
the man who could reasonably be described as the editor
of the Bible as we know it.

Chapter 23

This man went home again at rights with God.

It was the fashion at one time to sneer at the Catholic who
comes to confession and can do no more than repeat the same
list of half a dozen sins he has repeated many times before.
"My dear, how very boring! How can one make it more
interesting? Why not have a dialogue, in depth, on the
remote origins of people's hang-ups? Let's put the priest
in an armchair and the client in another and allow them
half an hour and then both of them will find it frightfully
interesting to work out where all those fascinating little
peccadilloes come from."

Ugh! Nothing could be more ill-advised.
Nothing would please the devil more
than to focus discussion on his handiwork.
Nothing could more completely contradict
what Jesus says in the Gospel.

Sin isn't a fascinating topic of conversation.
Sins aren't for analysis. Sins are for the dustbin.
Sins are to be forgiven and forgotten.

Sadly we live in a society where fashion accessories have
to include not only a personal stereo but a personal shrink
who can be relied on to find their clients as endlessly
fascinating as they do themselves.

Don't misunderstand me: I am not denigrating the work
of psychologists and psychiatrists, nor am I ignoring the
complexities of mental illness which need professional diagnosis.
I'm simply saying that the confessional isn't the psychiatrist's chair.

Radio 4 has been repeating several of the fascinating

programmes made over the years by Dr Anthony Clare –
in his psychiatrist's chair have sat the likes of Les Dawson,
Claire Rayner, Arthur Ashe. And they have all, as it were,
allowed their sessions to be bugged and later broadcast.
It allowed us to learn more about their problems, their
defence mechanisms and their courage in dealing with
their pasts. I do not knock such programmes where
they have the active consent of the participants.
But one would never bug a confessional and broadcast
its contents because the intention is totally different.

The psychiatrist is a well-trained expert, lending a helpful
question to tease out an individual's problem. The priest
deals with acknowledged sins by putting them in the past.
Even recurring sins. Their recurrence is put into the past.
Our greatest gift is today, and so yesterday is put in its place
and God's grace is invited in to flow around us in the present.

To a large extent the patient in the chair is defending
himself against perceptive questioning, justifying himself.
The penitent in confession has no need to do that. He can
safely leave justification to God: God knows everything
and is perfectly capable of understanding the origins of sins.
The penitent needs only to name the sin, not explain it,
and to beg forgiveness.

Sometimes – most times, being the creatures of habit we are –
the sins will come out like a list, a depressingly familiar list.
That's what one expects: sin is habit-forming and by definition
boring. We eradicate sins not by trying to enliven them with
interesting anecdotage but by acknowledging their existence
and asking God to forgive them.

The Pharisee came to the Temple to pray and his prayer is
an essay in self-congratulation reeking of pride and pomposity.
Clearly he lives at the centre of his universe.

The tax-collector came to apologise, and his prayer is a simple admission of failure. Clearly the centre of his universe is God.

And so the tax-collector will be a happier man than the Pharisee can ever be, because the tax-collector is always going to be overwhelmed by God's mercy and amazed by his grace. The Pharisee takes it for granted that God is grateful to have created such a one as he. One day he will discover how tediously self-centred he is and his mortification will be complete. The tax-collector tries each day and every day to do God's will, and because he persists despite the setbacks, one day he will find himself enfolded in God's arms and his joy will be complete.

I've heard quite a number of stories of children coming to confession and trying to invent sins to impress the priest. You have to smile – and I'm sure God has a sense of humour adequate for the purpose. Trying to be interesting in confession is something we can leave to the children. Trying to impress the confessor with fascinating defences of our sinfulness is something we can leave to the Pharisee.

Don't mock at the simple listing of sins.
In the honesty of the undefended indefensible
lies self-forgiveness and in the candour of the poor sinner
lies the doorway to God's forgiveness.

When we come to confession we are not providing material for an award-winning radio programme. We are come into God's house to speak tersely of our shame and to experience that mercy which is as gentle as silence.

God, be merciful to me, a sinner.

Chapter 24

Your faith has saved you.

Yes – but what sort of faith? Faith in what?
Are we just talking about the consequence of a miracle?
I think not. Miracles may be impressive, even persuasive,
but they're only indicators, never proof positive.

If Elisha cured Naaman of leprosy, if Jesus cured ten others,
it might signify no more than that they were both holy men,
prophets, faith-healers. The grateful Samaritan ex-leper is
the man we should focus on. He threw himself at the feet
of Jesus and thanked him because Jesus had been the agent
of his cure. But first, the leper turned back "praising God
at the top of his voice" – and that's the key to it.

That was what Jesus drew our attention to: "no-one else
has come back to give praise to God except this foreigner."
His priority was to praise God. So we're not really talking
about signs and wonders, indeed we remember that Jesus
denounced those who chased after miracles as being
a faithless generation. The faith we're talking about
is not conversion by a cure or miracle but a pure faith
in God, revealed in determination to praise God.

So our real subject today isn't amazement at miracles.
Our real subject is the faith in God that saves us. How do
we find and deepen such a faith? It's not an intellectual
process. Faith is not the conclusion of logic or even
the reward of moral probity. It is a gift from God
and neither I nor anyone else knows why God chooses
to give it to one person and not another. Faith is not
the inevitable outcome of an intellectual quest.
And that should be enough to awaken in us a respect

for other people's intellectual journeys.

"It is indeed a great question whether atheism is not
as philosophically consistent with the phenomena
of the physical world, taken by themselves,
as the doctrine of a creating or governing power."

Those aren't my words. They were preached in 1829
by John Henry Newman, then Vicar of St Mary's,
in Oxford. They acknowledge that it is intellectually
respectable to believe in a God or in atheism.
My friend's atheism does not impugn my intellectual
integrity any more than my Catholicism impugns
his intellectual integrity. To each of us, things may be
self-evident – but they may be different things.

Argument takes us a fair way along the road, but there
comes a point when I'm reminded of gallant old Aunt Eller
in *Oklahoma*! "... that's about as far as I can go."
So how does one press on further? I think by responding
to life's experiences and by being constantly open
to further insights.

Let me digress for a few moments. What is music?
To some it is an intellectual process chronicled on the staves
of a score. I remember a colleague of mine in Radio 3
who only rarely went to concerts and recitals because
he derived his real pleasure, not from the variable and
flawed performances but from contemplating the score
and hearing it internally.

Now that's not something I could do, not least because
I never learnt how to read music. I experience music
as a listener. I hear a sequence and a tapestry of sounds
emerging from my CD player, and my pleasure is in its
infinite variety. And I can either repeat the pleasure
by repeated listening to one CD or extend the pleasure
by listening to alternative recordings of the same work.

Is Krystian Zimmerman more impressive when he plays
the Chopin Concertos under Giulini or when he's both
soloist and conductor himself? A judgement can be made.

And then there is another dimension: the lone experience
of listening at home is a musical experience quite different
from the shared experience listening with others in a
concert hall.

A long time ago now, I was offered the chance of going
to Wagner's wonderful human comedy *The Mastersingers
of Nuremberg*. I nearly turned it down. I thought Wagner
was too loud and too long and too complex for the likes of me.
But then I was given the privilege of going to Sadlers Wells
and seeing and hearing and feeling it come to life under
the guidance of Reginald Goodall.

It was a road to Damascus experience. It fair knocked me off
my horse. I could hardly wait to go to later performances,
and as each one occurred my perceptions deepened.
Eventually I went to other places with other performers
and other conductors. I've bought four complete performances
on CD and I've experienced many *Meistersinger*. And that has
created a new reality within me: a conflation of experiences.
I now 'know' a sort of ideal *Meistersinger*: a perfect *Meistersinger*.
Perfect?! Well, in a way, yes.

I have never actually heard a complete perfect performance
but one exists in my mind, comprising elements from all the
things I've heard in many actual performances. I know
how each note and chord ought to sound, how each feeling
should be articulated. It exists – that perfect *Meistersinger* –
not perhaps in my mind, but in my heart or my soul.
It's in my heart that my love of *Meistersinger* enables me
to experience the optimum *Meistersinger*.

And so it is, I think, with God. When we first hear the idea
proposed, it may seem too deep, too complex, too unreal.

But then a particular experience, a moment of spiritual awareness will open up the possibility of understanding something which looked at first sight impenetrable.

And little by little, further actual experiences build up a more profound awareness. It doesn't come from reading words any more than music comes from reading scores. It's in the accumulation of experiences that an optimum idea emerges, not in the mind but in the heart or soul. We are enabled to know what music is by listening to it. We are enabled to know what love is by loving and being loved. And it is life itself that enables us to go beyond the intellectual arguments for God into an awareness of God in the heart and the soul.

Musicology does not necessarily lead to love of music. Philosophy does not necessarily lead to love of God. As Francis of Assisi memorably put it, "by love he can be gotten and holden, by thought never." We know this sort of process throughout our lives. I learnt what love is by loving. I learnt what music is by listening. I know a perfect *Meistersinger* through innumerable experiences of imperfect ones. And I know who God is through praising him, praying to him and appreciating him in the silence of my heart.

That's how faith comes. It's not amazement at miracles of healing or even the wonders of creation. Faith is the gift that comes when you open your heart to the possibility that it may be given. It might knock you off your horse as it did to Saul. It might open a new world as Goodall's *Mastersingers* did to me. And all the various and wonderful experiences of loving and being loved might bring into reality the God who is love.

That's the faith that saves us.

John Henry Cardinal Newman, 1801–1890

Sketch from life, 1883

This sermon was preached in Cardinal Newman's oratory at Littlemore, now looked after by the sisters of the Spiritual Family, The Work. The occasion was the anniversary of the day when the Blessed Sacrament was first reserved in that tiny historic room.

Chapter 25

You have kept the best wine till now.

When I was a boy I understood that guests had to be treated
with great hospitality. It was difficult; there was a war on.
Food was rationed. Even things like potatoes and cabbage
which we grew ourselves on the allotment were scarce.
So when visitors came it was F H B – family hold back.
That's all Mother had to say before guests arrived.
F H B. And so we did hold back.

I understand therefore what happened at Cana. The family
should have held back but they thought there would be plenty.
So they didn't. And there wasn't!
Disaster! The ignominy of running short of wine
at the reception. It would be just as awful today.

So why did Jesus intervene? Was he rebuking the family
for not holding back? Was he accepting the convention
that wedding guests needed to be made tipsy? Was he
giving his blessing to the institution of marriage?

I think his motive was actually very simple. His mother
certainly would have known all about F H B. She saw this
nice young couple in danger of becoming a laughing stock
among their friends. And she knew that Jesus wouldn't
want that. So she dug him in the ribs with her immaculately
sharp elbow and said: "They have no wine". Jesus pretended
to be slow on the uptake: "What's that got to do with me?"
Mary ignored him; she didn't argue or push it. A word
from her was enough. She just went over to the steward
and instructed him to do as he was told.

And so Jesus, true God and true man, used his divine power
for the first time for a miracle that looks ridiculous.

You'd have thought that his first demonstration of such
power would be deeply impressive: giving sight to the blind,
curing leprosy, feeding a multitude, even raising someone
from the dead. But no, what he was asked to do was to
replenish the vino. And he did. He had to change water
into wine. And he did.

And we have to ask ourselves why? Why a wedding?
Why such a superficial task for divine intervention?

To Jesus it clearly wasn't trivialising. The serenity of
a young couple on their big day mattered to him.

It should matter to us. We have all but priced our young
people out of weddings. We've made it such a social ordeal,
such an expense that many won't go for it. We should be
re-thinking weddings. Re-establishing the simple celebration.
Not a cast of thousands but the number we can entertain
without needing miracles.

The purpose of a wedding isn't to carouse with cohorts
of distant relations. Its purpose is to welcome Jesus into
the hearts and home of a couple who are eager to live life
to the full. Their love is strong. Their hopes are high.
They need God's blessing in good times and bad,
in sickness and in health.

So if Jesus is there, with them, from day one,
they can be sure that in all that life brings
they will certainly find the spiritual strength,
the moral power, the grace they need
to make the right choices.

When I hear that Gospel story it doesn't seem the least bit
trivial to me. It tells me that marriage requires the presence
of Christ, that married happiness springs from the grace of God.
We get all our values cock-eyed. We organise showy weddings.
We serve the best wine first to impress the Joneses.

We show off. We boast. We run into debt.
And the showier the wedding, the more likely
the marriage will come unstuck.

A couple. And Jesus. That's all it needs.
The best wine is the true presence of God
and it is Jesus who transforms the situation.
It is Jesus who gives the couple the tenacity,
the patience, the commitment, the energy,
the love they need to make a go of it.
The essence of a wedding is the presence
of Christ in the marriage. We understand that.

We are celebrating two anniversaries this morning.
It's the anniversary of the Community itself
and for each member of this community
Jesus is more than a guest. He is the bridegroom.
It is also the anniversary of the reservation of the
Blessed Sacrament in this historic and holy place –
and that is objectively, and for all of us, the Real Presence
of Christ among us. Jesus the Bridegroom; Jesus our guest;
the divine presence among us; *Dieu parmi nous.*

So we are acutely aware this morning that for us
he has kept the best wine. We will drink that eucharistic
wine of his Presence among us. And we will thank God
for his willingness, nay for his determination to be with us;
and for his sacramental way of demonstrating that he is
indeed with us.

Jesus the Bridegroom, Jesus the member of the Wedding.

There is for us no need for family to hold back.
He has filled our lives with his own presence;
he has filled our cup of happiness to overflowing.

Chapter 26

So that they may believe that it was you who sent me.

We read the story of the raising of Lazarus
and realise that there are questions to be asked.
We need to know why Jesus worked this miracle.

That it was a miracle is beyond doubt. Martha was horrified
when Jesus ordered them to take the stone away –
the corpse would have been rotting already.
But when Jesus called him, Lazarus returned to life –
feet and hands still bound with the grave cloths.

A miracle, undoubtedly. But why? Why would the Son of God
use his divine power to bring back to life someone who had died
of natural causes? Why intervene? In the case of the son of a
widow, Jesus saw the mother's distress and was moved by pity
for her, and raised her son to life and restored him to her.
We can understand compassion.

But Lazarus was no stranger. Jesus knew Martha and Mary well
and when their brother was struck down by illness,
the message they sent to Jesus said:
"Lord, the man you love is ill."
It was one of the most awkward decisions Jesus ever had to make.
Could he legitimately use his divine power on behalf of a friend?
Not if that were the only consideration.
But the people saw it as a test case.
If he can't intervene to do something for someone as worthy
as Lazarus, how can he do anything for anyone?

Jesus saw the situation as a test. It was first a test for Martha.
Clearly she had hoped, indeed expected, that Jesus would
intervene to cure Lazarus before he died, and she was bitterly
disappointed when Jesus failed to come.

She rebuked him: "If you'd been here, he wouldn't have died."
Jesus said tersely: "Your brother will rise again."
"Yes", said Martha flatly. "I know he'll rise again
at the resurrection on the last day."
"I *am* the resurrection", said Jesus gently, "do you believe this?"
"Yes", said Martha, "I believe that you are the Christ,
the Son of God."

And that declaration of faith was what Jesus needed to hear.
She was devastated by her brother's death –
but she was still prepared to proclaim Jesus as the Christ.

And so *before* Jesus made any intervention with divine power,
she had declared herself. Once the declaration had been made
that Jesus was the Lord of life and death, Jesus was free to prove it,
not to win her faith but to *justify* her faith and reward it.
The motive becomes clear.
You don't work a miracle to prove you are a miracle worker
but to reward faith.
The motive has to be pure.

Jesus rewards Martha, rewards the faith of Martha with the
miracle she thought had been denied her. She thought he'd
said 'No' to her prayer but still believed he was the Christ and
proclaimed her faith – and so he was free to restore life to her
brother, the friend he loved. And of course that seems natural –
if you love someone, you do your best for them. The people
who stood around needed to see Martha proclaim her faith
and then the miracle, and so to believe that it was God who
had sent him. It is Martha's order of priorities that matters.
Love, and faith. Trust apparently ignored.
But faith proclaimed even so. And faith rewarded.

Then the rest of us, seeing the miracle, ask why?
Fishes and loaves multiplied. Storms on the lake quelled.
The blind and the lame healed. Such things stop you in
your tracks and make you ask who on earth could do a thing

like that? Precisely so. Who on earth could do a thing like that?
It's the crunch question – because the answer has to be:
only God. And a fortiori who on earth could raise himself
from the dead? The final miracle is the ultimate miracle.
The dead body of Jesus, drained of blood, is buried and lies
in the tomb from Friday afternoon till Saturday is over
and then Jesus reappears. Not a ghost. A human being.

Who on earth could do a thing like that? Only God.
Why would he do a thing like that? He died to set us free.
He rose to prove we are free. He died for love, to prove
how far he was prepared to go to rescue us – he rose again
because love is ultimately more powerful than hate, and sin,
and death. He took on human nature to show it could be
perfectly good. He accepted death on the cross to prove
how far love would go. He rose from the dead so that
we might believe as Martha did that he is the resurrection
and the life.

We will die. But we will never die.
Our mortal death will kill the body
but we have a divine spark which can never be quenched
and which – in the fullness of time – will ensure
that just as Jesus was restored to life in his glorious risen body,
so will we be.

We look for the resurrection of the dead and the life
of the world to come. Amen

Chapter 27

And do not put us to the test.

While I was away in Ireland my diary went missing,
and one of the places where it might have been removed
was when I left it on the passenger seat while I was filling up
at the petrol station, and had left the door unlocked.

The diary actually turned up somewhere else completely, but
what was interesting to me was that the garage man was able to
play back for me the cctv tape. It covered the whole forecourt
and established that no one had approached the car while I was
inside the shop paying. Very useful to be able to rule out
that possibility.

We're so used to cctv now – all over the place.
If you're an honest citizen going about legitimate business
it's no problem. In some situations it's a real advantage.

I read yesterday about its use in the Gower Bird Hospital
in Wales. When birds come in to them with broken wings,
injured feet, wounded eyes, they now put the hurt birds
into an area monitored by cctv.

Why is that a help? It's because if an injured bird can see
anyone watching it, it will do its best to conceal its injury
and put on a façade of normality. It knows that in the natural
world a predator would target an injured bird as easy prey.
And so, if they're aware of being watched, they'll consciously
hide the problem and pretend nothing's wrong. But once
an injured bird is left alone, it'll relax and slump into a more
comfortable position, dropping a painful wing, closing
a sore eye, taking the weight off a hurt leg. And so the vets
watching on cctv can diagnose what's really wrong.

I think it's not only birds that cover up their injuries.
We do the same. We call it the stiff upper lip.
We pretend nothing's wrong, we walk tall and only
in the privacy of our own room do we nurse ourselves
and try to heal. It's true of our physical selves
and it's true of our spiritual selves.

We practice the faith, we go to the services,
we live in the aura of religious convention,
and only in our private thoughts do we admit to ourselves
our spiritual hurts and doubts.

We are bereaved; we are lonely; we are unhappy in love;
we're aware we're wasting our lives –
but we couldn't possibly admit anything like that
to anyone else. And that is a pity
because there is one healing agent who can help us.

In a sense, he has closed circuit television– he can see
not only our deeds but our thoughts; he can read us,
and diagnose our problems, for he is the great physician –
the One who wants us to be whole.

And that is why in our spiritual lives
we need to look to the honesty and integrity of our prayers.
It's no use putting on a façade of faith if it's not genuine.

Much better to admit a doubt. It's deliberate deception
if we parade our strength when deep inside we know
we're weak. It's so much wiser to be honest.
In the privacy of our own hearts, in the honesty of
our real feelings, we have to remember that Eternal Vet
who literally died to set us free and whose prime concern
is to deal with our hurts. It's in our prayers that we can
safely say the truth and admit our hurt and our vulnerability.

Some people try to use doctors, psychiatrists, counsellors –
agents outside ourselves. But that's always suspect, because

of our self-centredness. We want the doctor's sympathy,
we want the psychiatrist to recognise how fascinating we are,
we want counsellors to short-circuit the ups and downs of life –
and these are often unreal, selfish tactics and get us nowhere.
In the last analysis we do best when we speak only to God
and speak the whole truth.

The characteristic of the saints
is that they understand themselves
with no illusions, no pretence, no romanticising –
but it doesn't depress them
because they also understand
how profoundly God loves them.

No self-absorption, no self-pity, no rose-tinted spectacles –
the honesty of being alone and unwatched
but with that huge extra bonus of awareness
of that cctv which is God seeing us.

We speak to him as a Father and we praise him.
We identify him as the provider of our daily sustenance
and ask his help. And in that final act of confidence
in him we admit our vulnerability and ask him to deliver
us from evil. And do not put us to the test.

In the innermost corners of our being the healer sees
what is really wrong with us and heals with his love.

Dying on the cross, Jesus knew that he had redeemed humanity:"It is accomplished." The Calvary on the altar of St John's College, Oxford.

Photograph taken by Fr Cormac in 1960.

Chapter 28

All I have is yours and all you have is mine.

Jesus spoke those words to God his Father
immediately before he set off for the Garden of Gethsemane
on the night his Passion began. His prayer was
that he would be enabled to give eternal life
to all those entrusted to him by the Father.

And in the last moments of his life, dying on the cross,
Jesus knew he had succeeded: "It is accomplished."

What was his achievement? It was to eclipse absolutely
everything in the world that relates to sin and death.
The supreme sacrifice of the Son of God ended the alienation
of humanity from the love of God. His love for the Father
is all-engulfing and it sweeps us along too. The Father sent him
not just to preach love, not just to live a life of love,
but to die for love. What we see and understand when
we look at the crucifix is that the Son of God would go
to any lengths to prove his love and do his Father's will.
It is our awareness of that which makes us Christians.

I remember once asking my Mother "Do we have to go to
Mass?" And she looked at me and said "No. Not if you
think there's anything else that would do you more good."
She was right. Coming to Mass isn't a boring social duty.
She saw with complete clarity that for us to be present at
that act of sacrifice, when God's love is made visible on
Calvary, is to receive all the strength of mind and heart and
spirit that comes out of our awareness. We draw strength
to live our lives from our awareness of our eternal life.

It's been a beautiful spring this year – there have been many days when even the most doddery of us have felt sprightly and cheerful, when the poor old world looked capable of revival. It would be a real saddo who couldn't find some encouragement in the blossom and the new leaves and the *freshness deep down things*. But there is a problem. Nature goes in an ever-repeating cycle: spring, summer, autumn, winter – and then spring again. But for humanity, for us, there is only one cycle: the spring and summer of each life give way to autumn and declining winter. In a human life there is no second spring.

In the salad days of our life a young man falls in love and says he'll always love, and probably means it. But he is fortune's fool, and there is no 'always.' In his initial intoxication with love it never occurs to him that others can be fickle. In his first encounter with freedom of spirit it never occurs to him that anger can poison the human heart and that rage and brutality can overwhelm individual freedom. In his love-sick relationship it never occurs to him that her beauty fades and his strength weakens.

But that's the truth of it. To each one of us is given a single spring, a summer, an autumn, a winter. The duration of each sector of life will vary from person to person but there is only the one cycle. It will do us no good to rage against the fading of the light. All of us hope for a long life and fruitfulness, but we know that it may happen, it may not. So we have to live life with a strategy that will make the most of every second.

It is no accident that Christianity contradicts the seasons of Nature. When winter has shrunk the hours of daylight to short days of chilly bleakness, Christianity celebrates a Birthday. When spring returns to fill nature with exuberance and to make men dizzy with longing, Christianity mourns for a death.

Christianity runs counter to the recurring cycle of nature.
The death on Calvary turns out not to be the same as the
cyclical death of the earth, but a triumphant breaking-out
from that annual cycle and a transition to an everlasting life.

The seasons belong to time but we properly belong to eternity.
The roller-coaster of the seasons will go on long after we are dead –
and there are those who take comfort from the thought
that our bones, our ashes, form part of some cosmic recycling.

What the Resurrection did for us was to cut right across
that seasonal pattern of the natural world and to alter
our lives completely: one small step for a man,
one giant leap for mankind.

When Jesus of Nazareth stepped out of the tomb on Easter
morning we leapt with him towards our eternity. And that
changes everything. I can now deal with my own ration of life:
I can look back to my spring with affection and amusement.
I can look back on my summer with gratitude and some surprise.
I am living my autumn with eagerness and equanimity and
I contemplate winter with no discontent and some serenity,
because I know that when my one single cycle of life is over,
I hope for that eternity beyond,
that unquenchable love where death has no dominion.

All I have is yours, and all you have is mine;
and in them I am glorified.

A baptism is always a celebration of the Christian family. Georgia O'Hare was baptised by Fr Cormac in St Chad's Cathedral, Birmingham. Here she is with her parents Michael and Julie, and her two sets of grandparents. Fr Cormac said the Requiem Mass for Michael O'Hare senior (on the right) in the Old Chapel in Newry on 14 July 2004. The sermon is printed opposite.

Chapter 29

They recognised him in the breaking of the bread.

We are here at a Requiem Mass. It's a time of deep sorrow,
but also an occasion when our faith proclaims Resurrection.
Requiem means rest, the rest from labour which comes
at the end of a working life, and release from the constraints
of physical frailty.
Rest – as a reward for a life well-lived.

We can remember Cardinal Newman's prayer:
> May he support us all the day long,
> Till the shades lengthen and the evening comes
> And the busy world is hushed
> And the fever of life is over
> And our work is done.
> Then in his mercy may he give us a safe lodging
> and a holy rest and peace at the last.

But 'rest' has another meaning as well: the rest of life.
Death is not a terminus, but the great turning-point of life.
At the moment of death our life is changed, not ended.
And the lifetime we have experienced thus far is tiny
compared with the eternal life that lies ahead.

This short and measurable earthly existence
which we have been living out is simply the prologue,
which takes place, brightly-lit, in front of a gauze
and at this moment of transition, it fades into
the wide unmeasurable life beyond the gauze.
In a very real sense, the rest is yet to come.
Our thoughts today, here in this place,
are not of the extinguishing of an existence
but of the opening-out of a narrow human lifespan

into the warm radiance of eternity.

The last time I saw Michael he was clearly not in the best
of health; but he and Vera had come over to give me support
on 14 September, my final Sunday in my parish
before going into retirement. And I deeply appreciated
his willingness to make that journey.
It's as if they were standing-in for my own parents.

I first met him as a Dad, the father of two much-admired
dancers, and I marvelled then, and many times since,
at how willingly he gave of his own time and his own life
to support and encourage them.
As I got to know him better, I understood
that it wasn't just a sense of duty that impelled him
but a tremendous generosity of heart.
I was always aware of both those elements in Michael:
duty and generosity. He knew very clearly
what he was duty-bound to do and he clearly loved
what his generous heart wanted him to do.

He and Vera came to my diaconate ordination in Camden Town
in 1987 and to my ordination to the priesthood in Westminster
Cathedral in 1988, and I have treasured the memories
of consequent events, most notably the wedding
of Michael and Julie and the baptism of Georgia.
Is it any wonder that I feel greatly privileged
to be celebrating this Requiem Mass for him.
The Mass was at the heart of his faith and I chose the Gospel
of the supper at Emmaus because of that.

The apostles had followed Jesus with varying levels of
enthusiasm until the events of Good Friday seemed to imply
a terrible delusion. They scattered in panic and desolation,
unable to see in the dead Jesus anything beyond a catastrophic
tragedy. Their simplistic little construct of beliefs collapsed
like a house of cards. Death had, after all, rung down

the curtain on the life of Jesus. Death is destruction
and oblivion, and death had won.

Until the Easter event, three days later.
It wasn't at all what they were expecting. Those disciples,
on the road to Emmaus, slunk along, their spirits dejected,
their heads bent, too overwhelmed by disappointment
to see who had joined them on their journey.
It was only at the breaking of bread that they recognised
the Jesus who was risen and had returned to live among them.
A man from whose body every drop of blood had drained
was now visibly alive again, talking with them,
walking alongside them and explaining what it all meant.

The breaking of bread at this Mass continues their recognition
of the Risen Lord. And the resurrection of Jesus shows
that experience – beyond the gauze of death –
which will be the resurrection of all of us.
In the light of Easter we do not need to mourn for Michael.
We recognise our own sorrow at his departure,
but we see that we will follow him into that radiant eternity.
All his human limitations are now transcended.
He now understands what he could not understand before,
he now loves more powerfully than he ever could before,
he now exists more fulfilled than he ever was before.
For the rest of his life, which is open-ended and open-hearted,
he can see this world as God sees it
and he can revel in loving it as God loves it.

That's what we mean by that familiar phrase 'the communion
of saints' – the ability to share the vision of God himself,
and to revel in limitless love of all God's creation.

When we pray today for his eternal rest,
we don't mean the passive experience of a long sleep;
we mean being fully alive,
revelling in a freedom to love as never before.

Chapter 30

This very night the demand will be made for your soul.

What a lop-sided, unfair world this is.
We see the man who has worked hard – laborious days,
cares of office, sleepless nights – having the fruits of his labour
snatched away by someone who hasn't worked at all.

What's the point of doing all the right things
if someone who does all the wrong things gets ahead of us?
We have a rather simplistic expectation that the injustices
of this world will be sorted in the next. It's something
you often hear: he missed out on all the good things of this life –
he'll be recompensed in heaven!
That's not piety: that's just greed postponed.

Remember Jesus's story of the rich man and the beggar?
The rich man thought that money could buy anything
and was very put out when it failed to buy him long life.
And then he saw the beggar Lazarus resting in heaven
while he himself was dying of thirst in the other place.
He didn't ask himself: how have I gone so wrong?
He still thinks he can bribe Lazarus to bring him a drink!
The penny never dropped that what was wrong was that
he thought his happiness depended on his own affluence.
Even when death overtook him he still didn't get it.

What matters isn't our gains and profits – it's how generous
we are, how full of love, how skilful we become in giving joy
to others. If we see Heaven as the place where the Boss
gets even with those who've done us down, if we see Heaven
as the belated recognition of all our virtues, we've totally
missed the point. It's still greed, it's still ambition,
it's still centred on me, me, me.

Jesus warns us – don't look to God to be a sort of umpire
who will sort out our opponents; don't see him as a lawyer
specializing in compensation claims.
Be on your guard, says Jesus, against avarice of any sort.
A man's life isn't made secure by what he owns –
even when he has more than he needs.
It's not what he owns that brings fulfilment;
it's what he gives that brings happiness.

At the end of Cole Porter's great musical *Anything Goes*,
the beautiful heroine turns down marriage with a wealthy
English Lord and marries the young and handsome but
impecunious hero. Her Mom is not best pleased by this
overturning of her plans: "We're going to be poor again –
I shall have to spend the rest of my life living in hotels."
A filthy-rich Wall Street financier comes to Mom's rescue.
Since he sold his shares he's become so rich he can buy
anything he likes – so marry him! At which point the
hero has to confess that he had failed to sell those shares
as his boss had instructed and the tycoon crumbles:
"I'm ruined." Mom backs off at the speed of light.
Then a dramatic telegram reveals that the shares
which should have been sold have now gone through
the roof, and he's a zillionaire. Mom rushes eagerly
towards him to live affluently ever after!

It's great fun; the satire is delightful and de-lovely and
one's mind goes back to the great show-stopper earlier on:
Blow Gabriel Blow. Cole Porter's fictional lady evangelist
is right on message and echoes today's Gospel very effectively.
Even zillionaires have to die – and where are their zillions then?

The comforts of the rich man have no staying power.
God said to him: "Fool, this very night the demand
will be made for your soul." And all those hoarded dollars
have no value on the other side of the Styx.

Heaven isn't rewards or compensation.
Heaven is where the generous of heart feel at home.
Those who live their life on earth in greed and resentment
experience a hell of their own creation.
And the ones who find themselves in heaven
are those who on earth forgot themselves
and derived their happiness from their generosity to others.
They discover that all the time
they were sharing all they had to make others happy,
they were actually making themselves rich
in the sight of God.

What do all the stocks and shares add up to?
What avail all the worldly ambitions?
What does all that matter when you hear
the unpredictable sound of the last trump?

> Do you hear that playing?
> Do you know *who's* playing?
> Why it's Gabriel, Gabriel playing –
> will you be ready to go
> when I blow my horn?

Cole Porter's evangelist, chic and glamorous as she is,
is preaching precisely the same message as John the Baptist
in the wilderness. Repent! Have a change of heart
while you still can.

> Once I was ready for hell . . .
> but I said "Satan, farewell."
> Now I'm all ready to fly,
> yes to fly higher and higher and higher.
> I've purged my soul and my heart too
> and climb up the mountain top and start to blow –
> I want to join your happy band
> And play all day in the promised land
> So blow Gabriel blow.

That's the vibrant language of the musical
translating into twentieth-century terms
the timeless optimism we heard in our responsorial psalm:

>   let us come before him, giving thanks;
>   with songs let us hail the Lord.

If, this very night, the demand is made for our soul,
if, this very night, Gabriel should blow his horn,
may we experience heaven
as the homecoming for the generous-hearted.